COMMON
SENSE
BUSINESS

COMMON
SENSE
BUSINESS

PRINCIPLES FOR PROFITABLE LEADERSHIP

THEODORE ROOSEVELT MALLOCH
AND WHITNEY MACMILLAN

Skyhorse Publishing

Skyhorse Publishing books may be purchased in bulk at special discounts for sales promotion, corporate gifts, fund-raising, or educational purposes. Special editions can also be created to specifications. For details, contact the Special Sales Department, Skyhorse Publishing, 307 West 36th Street, 11th Floor, New York, NY 10018 or info@skyhorsepublishing.com.

Skyhorse® and Skyhorse Publishing® are registered trademarks of Skyhorse Publishing, Inc.®, a Delaware corporation.

Visit our website at www.skyhorsepublishing.com.

10 9 8 7 6 5 4 3 2 1

Library of Congress Cataloging-in-Publication Data is available on file.

Cover design by Mark Karich

ISBN: 978-1-5107-2981-0
Ebook ISBN: 978-1-5107-2982-7

Printed in the United States of America

TABLE OF CONTENTS

Part III: Applying Common Sense

ACCOLADES FOR *COMMON-SENSE BUSINESS*

Every business person, in fact, every person, needs to consider the purpose and significance of their life and enterprise. *Common-Sense Business* offers such a compass.

—James Amos, former CEO of Mail Boxes Etc.

A *magnum opus* written in simple words and built on real-life cases, reminding every modern person what a cardinal virtue they have easily forgotten while searching in vain for "solutions."

—Fanglu Wang, chairman, CITIC Capital (China)

Empowering business to serve the common good demands new ways of thinking about how to do strategy and make decisions. Ted Malloch and Whitney MacMillan provide a powerful idea in *Common-Sense Business* that has the potential to transform how all companies are run, to the benefit of shareholders, employees, and communities alike. Nothing could be more valuable!

—Mark Drewell, CEO,
Globally Responsible Leadership Initiative

Thus far we have seen value only in *smart* organizations. This book shifts the paradigm by moving the focus from smart to *wise*. We all need to seriously relearn from this book.

—Jitin Goyal, president,
Banking and Financial Services, Virtusa Polaris

Here is a book that is at the same time brave, deep, stirring, and practical. It is brave because it dares to speak unfashionable truths about economics, companies, and society. It is deep because it tackles philosophical issues raised by Aristotle, Aquinas, and Kant. It doesn't just stir us up and call us to rise from our weak-kneed conformity; it is also practical, because it offers us a whole range of tools with which we can spring into action!

—Prabhu Guptara, executive director,
Organizational Development, Wolfsberg (Switzerland)

This book should inspire all whom Pope Francis called the *remansado*, the people who move with kindness and humility. When we seem to be educating young MBAs to shoot faster than their shadow, this book makes a *very* compelling case to educate them to be courageous leaders, who are conscious of their decisions and that these decisions affect other people and our environment. This exceptionally good book comes just in time to help us so-called risk adversers to gain confidence and to start demanding to be called *sensibles*.

—Juan Pablo, Cerda CEO, TECO (Chile)

This is a most fascinating book on the much-needed transformation of economics and business from its materialistic, selfish, and reductionist form to a humanistic, prudent, and qualitative form. *Common-Sense Business* is required reading for businesspeople and economists—as well as for all students of these disciplines.

—Laszlo Zsolnai, professor and director,
Business Ethics Center, Corvinus University Budapest (Hungary),
and president, European SPES Institute, Leuven (Belgium)

This masterwork is a prime example of how to use corporate responsibility so as to reinvest in our young, talented, and gifted leaders of tomorrow. That alone reinforces its impact, which is here to stay!

—Karen Melonie Gould, author,
Happy Entrepreneur Mind Set

Primum non nocere. "First, do no harm": no harm to others, no harm to the earth, and no harm to oneself. This basic principle dictated by practical wisdom has been totally forgotten by the business world—as Ted Malloch and Whitney MacMillan show brilliantly—and replaced by a Promethean drive to unlimited profit at any cost . . . to others and to the earth. Already, the ancients had understood that Prometheus—the business leader—was to be chained, because once let loose, he would put fire to the universe.

—Antonin Pujos, president,
French Directors Institute (France)

This book is equally as enlightening as it is instructive. From philosophical foundations and real-world examples, *Common-Sense Business* derives conclusions and offers a set of tools for responsible business conduct with striking clarity.

—Ernst von Kimakowitz, founder and director,
Humanistic Management Center

This spectacularly insightful book identifies how recklessness has led us to the brink of disaster—and how to fix it. Every responsible executive needs common sense in business.

—Dr. Paul Zak, founding director,
Center for Neuroeconomics Studies

The ancients understood the importance of virtue for a flourishing society. While today, information and know-how are often used as substitutes, this book provides a compelling case for placing the critical virtue of prudence at the centre of the global economy.

—Peter S. Heslam, director,
Transforming Business, University of Cambridge

The fruit of our increasingly morally relativistic culture is clear: financial collapse, scandal, and corruption. This book uncovers the roots of good business, challenging and equipping the reader with practical guides to lead teams and build businesses on a solid foundation with transformational value. *Common-Sense Business* is an intellectual and practical guide for leaders who understand that as humans, in everything we do, we are meant to live holistic lives—as integral members of a community and enriched with meaning and purpose.

—Jinyoung Lee Englund, vice president,
Digital Currency Council

A brilliant and very robust reminder of the risks incurred by everyone when business leaders are left without guidance and give up prudence and practical wisdom for hubris and unlimited profits. We need to replace fear and greed with common sense and the common good, as this book so thoroughly documents.

—Christopher Wasserman, founding president,
Zermatt Summit Foundation (Switzerland)

Common-Sense Business is one of those special books that look backwards in order to help us look forward, and it does so in a winsome and winning way. Drawing on some of history's greatest minds, *Common-Sense Business* gives *practical* answers to the questions asked by Occupy Wall Street, the Tea Party, and others disillusioned with global businesses that have become detached from common sense and civic responsibility.

—David W. Miller, director,
Princeton University Faith & Work Initiative

Common-Sense Business is a great read. I like the way it blends philosophical discussions with examples of good and bad practice. It deserves to have very wide coverage and serious attention.

—Colin Mayer, Peter Moores Professor of Management Studies,
Saïd Business School, University of Oxford

For Betty and Beth
Our anchors in common sense and affection

PREFACE

In the words of French novelist Victor Hugo, the future has many names:

> For the weak it is the *unattainable*.
> For the fearful it is the *unknown*.
> For the bold it is the *opportunity*.

This bold book on common-sense business behavior aims to be the latter, for it represents and opens up opportunities for a most positive and practical way forward.

A number of years ago, I was introduced to a true gentleman and business legend named Whitney MacMillan. At the time, he was chairman and CEO of Cargill, the world's largest privately held company, a global giant in agribusiness. Whitney had a reputation as a strict but caring leader and as a no-nonsense player. He ran a tight ship and was focused beyond belief. Because we shared a similar Scottish background and a lifelong devotion to Presbyterian values and "work ethic," we hit it off. Whitney has clearly had a profound effect on worldwide business thinking about supply chains and commodities, but I came to appreciate the subtler side of his considerable business acumen.

I actually first met Whitney in New York City in 1979 at the Institute for East-West Security Studies (founded and run by the late John Mroz, who had a knack for bringing people together from different worlds). Whitney later came to chair the Institute, and our paths crossed more often at various annual meetings, in dialogues with Soviet dissidents and economists, and on trips to places like Poland and the USSR. We met together with the foreign minister of West Germany, Herr Hans-Dietrich Genscher, and with top brass from the Kremlin. I can still remember Whitney chairing a large meeting in Stockholm in 1990, where leading thinkers from the United States, Europe, and the USSR discussed economic reforms before the Berlin Wall came down. Some might even say such meetings helped foment the changes that were coming to pass, including the dramatic end of the Cold War.

I then encountered Whitney and his charming wife, Betty, at Yale University, where he was a significant donor and I was on the board and then later on the faculty. His philanthropic acuity matched his business sensibility, and the MacMillan Center for International and Area Studies at Yale testifies to this.

On a number of occasions, I had the benefit to interact with Whitney in closed circles. There he spoke his mind and often proved to be a contrarian and a very formidable thinker, both practically and conceptually. In the Bahamas, we met under the rubric of the Templeton Foundation to consider the nature of venture philanthropy. In Ojai, California, with the Liberty Fund, we discussed the contours of a generous society and the responsibility of business in a free-market culture. Whitney was never shy, even if he listened as much as he spoke. He exuded a kind of Midwestern common sense that was rooted in integrity and while kindly, demonstrated real authenticity. He was not a foolish or showy man, and he knew his business inside-out and outside-in, as few CEOs do.

When I approached him about this book, he was candid and said he would think about it with Betty, always ably by his side. I respected that and sent him a lengthy, detailed proposal and some texts from my earlier books, with which he was already familiar.

In September of last year, while in the United Kingdom on business (inspecting a chicken processing factory), Betty and Whitney came to our house in Woodstock, outside Oxford, and joined my wife, Beth, and I for a most delightful grouse dinner at *The Feathers* restaurant, a traditional Cotswold favorite. It was all rather pleasant and conversational. I didn't hear from Whitney for a few months, and my curiosity about his disposition toward the book idea piqued. Then on New Year's Eve, at about 11 p.m. GMT, I got a text on my iPhone. It was from Whitney, and it simply stated that Betty and he had decided to move ahead on this project and were fully supportive. We would meet numerous times thereafter to talk, collect ideas, and fashion our arguments. I learned a great deal about common sense and about "the Cargill way" in these exchanges.

It has been my true joy to have such an ally in this venture. And together, we aim to present a book accessible and enjoyable to readers from all walks of life—not just high-powered corporate. Our project brings together a number of strands of thinking that pertain to every sector of society and business—but they all center upon the virtue and practice of prudence. (In fact, our original working title for the book *was* "Prudence.") While prudence is still a highly esteemed virtue in some realms of society, it is particularly to the economic field that this asset must be reintroduced.

This is because prudent behavior, framed by common sense, has largely left both the business vocabulary and the parlance of everyday thinking in economics. That is a shame. We think it must be rediscovered in order to reorient business toward a better future where human flourishing is sustainably at the center of enterprise. It *can* again be habituated in good business practices and systems, and it is our intention not only to restore prudence to its rightful role but also to provide a rationale—complete with case-study illustrations and helpful tools—that can begin to move companies back in this right and good common-sense direction.

That's why at the end of this book you will find a number of audits, some exercises, and the Virtue Matrix, which are of practical use to any company, large or small, public or private, in any industry, and in any region of the world. We'd like your feedback on how these arguments and these tools have specifically benefited your business.

When we had to choose a cover for this book, like many authors, we were conflicted. We found the perfect characterization, though, as we chanced upon a suitable icon that was "hidden in plain sight"—as so many things in life often are. The very parchment of Thomas Paine's tract on *Common Sense*, so important to American history, seemed apt. It represents both a value firmly rooted in the virtue of prudent, diligent, honest work and a demonstration of viable stewardship—the American founding. Nothing could be more fitting to symbolize what we believe is still necessary centuries later: prudent business, based in common sense, that sustainably enriches humanity from sea to shining sea (and beyond).

This notion of economic stewardship implies a responsibility that humans have been charged with to care for all of the gifts ("resources" is the word the moderns would use) that we have been given, so as to preserve and pass them on to others and to future generations. In essence, it all boils down to trust; we humans, even in our business lives, are trustees.

Theodore Roosevelt Malloch and Whitney MacMillan
December 2016
Wayzata, Minnesota

OBITUARY FOR COMMON SENSE

Lori Borgman[1]

ommon Sense, a.k.a. C.S., lived a long life but died from heart failure at the brink of the millennium. No one really knows how old he was; his birth records were long ago entangled in miles and miles of bureaucratic red tape. Known affectionately to close friends as Horse Sense and Sound Thinking, he selflessly devoted himself to a life of service in homes, schools, hospitals, and offices, helping folks get jobs done without a lot of fanfare, whooping, and hollering.

Rules and regulations and petty, frivolous lawsuits held no power over C.S. A most reliable sage, he was credited with cultivating the ability to know when to come in out of the rain, the discovery that the early bird gets the worm, and how to take the bitter with the sweet.

C.S. also developed sound financial policies (don't spend more than you earn), reliable parenting strategies (the adult is in charge, not the kid), and prudent dietary plans (offset eggs and bacon with a little fiber and orange juice).

A veteran of the Industrial Revolution, the Great Depression, the Technological Revolution, and the Smoking Crusades, C.S. survived sundry cultural and educational trends including disco, the men's movement, body piercing, whole language, and new math. C.S.'s health began declining in the late 1960s when he became infected with the If-It-Feels-Good, Do-It virus.

In the following decades, his waning strength proved no match for the ravages of overbearing federal and state rules and regulations and an oppressive tax code. C.S. was sapped of strength and the will to live as the Ten Commandments became contraband, criminals received better treatment than victims, and judges stuck their noses in everything from Boy Scouts to professional baseball and golf.

His deterioration accelerated as schools implemented zero-tolerance policies. Reports of six-year-old boys charged with sexual harassment for kissing classmates, a teen suspended for taking a swig of Scope mouthwash after lunch, girls suspended for possessing Midol, and an honor student expelled for having a table knife in her school lunch were more than his heart could endure.

As the end neared, doctors say C.S. drifted in and out of logic but was kept informed of developments. Finally, upon hearing about a government plan to ban inhalers from 14 million asthmatics due to a trace of a pollutant that may be harmful to the environment, C.S. breathed his last.

Services will be at Whispering Pines Cemetery. C.S. was preceded in death by his wife, Discretion; one daughter, Responsibility; and one son, Reason. He is survived by two step-brothers, Half-Wit and Dim-Wit.

Memorial contributions may be sent to the Institute for Rational Thought. Farewell, Common Sense. May you rest in peace.

NOTES

1. Lori Borgman, "The Death of Common Sense," blog post (March 15, 1998), *loriborgman.com.*

INTRODUCTION

The only thing a person can never have too much of is common sense.

—Kathryn Smith

Early on the freezing cold morning of January 10, 1776, in Philadelphia, a forty-seven-page booklet was published that would go on to change American and indeed world history. It was the watershed moment in the American Revolution. The publication was called *Common Sense*, and its author was Thomas Paine. The arguments contained in the petite volume galvanized opposition to the Crown and catalyzed the political movement to independence.

Paine had been born in Britain and had only immigrated to America in 1774 at the suggestion of Benjamin Franklin. Writing for the *Pennsylvania Magazine* under the pseudonyms of Atlanticus, Aesop, and Vox Populi, he lashed out at the folly and wrongs of British rule. His common-sense opus, written in language every common person could understand, had instant and dramatic effect. Striking a chord with colonist conscience, it was rapidly translated into many languages, reprinted thousands of times over, and circulated widely. It did nothing less than convince Americans who were undecided on the issue of independence that they should unite and separate.

Paine considered the content of his pamphlet to be a plain truth (which was, at first, his working title), clear to all right-thinking, rational persons. He had borrowed the phrase from its earlier use in England (as early as the fourteenth century), where it was considered a sense very much like our other senses. They were called the "five wits," and the "common" sense united them into a useful whole.

Like that powerful expression of the American consciousness, today we need another jolt of common sense—this time in business. We need it to restore faith in the market and wealth creation and also to give common people, regular business men and woman in America and around the world, a prudent voice for creating a better future.

Unfortunately, it is often said that common sense is not as common as it ought to be. Possibly the best recent spokesperson for common sense was Ronald Reagan. In his farewell address, the fortieth president defined his time in office as "a rediscovery of our values and our common sense." Actually from the very start of his career, Reagan dedicated his tenure to his belief in the idea that society "could be operated efficiently by using the same common sense practiced in our everyday life, in our homes, in business and private affairs."

Today, some decades later, responsible, purposeful business leaders are taking up this mantle and laying claim to the phrase "common-sense business." What exactly does this mean, and how does it work? What truths do we hold as self-evident in a common-sense framework, and what are the benefits—to leaders, employees, shareholders, and communities, and most critically to companies themselves?

In the field of economics, common-sense behavior has been seen as saving more money when one is faced with an uncertain future; it's part of "risk aversion." The so-called precautionary saving motive is one of many faulty principles of this dismal science. In economics' cousin, accounting, prudence is a fundamental concept. It determines the time at which revenue can be recognized, which is not an unimportant or inconsequential event. Lawyers also still abide by the "prudent man rule," a nearly two-hundred-year-old judgment method appealing to common sense. Some governments have even established prudential conduct authorities, intended to guide fiscal choices in a better direction after the financial crisis.

Arguably the most dominant organization on the planet, the Catholic Church has insisted on maintaining the virtue of prudence in all ventures, making it part of its standard for belief and practice, the *Catechism*: "Prudence is the virtue that disposes practical reason to discern our true good in every circumstance and to choose the right means of achieving it."[1] It goes on to conclude with some sound advice: "The prudent man looks where he is going."[2]

If prudent behavior is right reason in action—or as we define it, the natural intelligence that is available to all rational people doing business—then why has it been mostly abandoned, forfeited in more recent times and nearly totally forgotten by our postmodern culture and governments? (That is, except for Reagan, and now President Trump.) Let's trace the history of common sense's demise, for in so doing, we can discover avenues for its possible resurrection.

Where We Lost Common Sense

I hope you enjoyed reading Lori Borgman's "obituary" at the front of this book. What she put cleverly into words around the turn of the recent century had been happening for many more years before that. Let's start with a hero of common sense, Aristotle.

For Aristotle, any conception of "the good life" employed practical wisdom. This wisdom, put into action, was prudence, and it was a virtue rooted not in meditation but experience. According to Aristotle, experience teaches us how to relate universal truths to particular situations, and it underscores the variety of individual circumstance. Wisdom leads to prudence, which leads to action, which leads to experience and more wisdom.

As social beings, humans act. (Sociologists call us "actors," because that's what we do.) We achieve certain ends and do so in conjunction with other ends, pursuing the state of wellness that Aristotle knew as *eudemonia*. In his *Nicomachean Ethics*, he stated, "Prudence is that virtue of the understanding which enables men to come to wise decisions about the relation to happiness of the goods and evils."

Nine hundred years later, *phronesis* was the Latin translation of prudence (common sense) for Thomas Aquinas and other Church fathers as they incorporated Aristotelian ideas into their theological framework and moral theology.

By the time of Thomas Hobbes, however, at the start of the modern era, we witness a complete rejection of such thinking. Hobbes rejected prudence as a proper concept in philosophy, casting it aside as mere conjecture. This turned ethics on its head, as prudence was demoted from a virtue to a tattered theory.

During the Scottish Enlightenment, Adam Smith (first and foremost a moral philosopher, and later the founder of economics) tried to revivify prudence and reconnect it to morality. An entire section of his opus, *The Theory of Moral Sentiments*, is devoted to the virtue of prudence as a form of common sense. The heavy influence of Stoicism can be seen in Smith's contribution to the concept of prudence. He saw it as an aspect of self-command or self-control over one's desires and emotions. Thinking as he did about the rising wealth of nations, Smith envisioned using prudence to make men "fit for society." The virtues of a sound economy for him corresponded to those of the "prudent man." Prudence was thus transformed back into a virtue—this time both economic and moral.

Today, however, prudence/common sense is hardly the supreme virtue it once was, if it is held as a virtue at all. This may be in part because we have abandoned the idea of a *telos*, a noble purpose guiding our actions into the future, in most of business and public life. Moral norms have been relativized and separated from both personal and business decisions. Prudence as an intellectual practice, signifying an excellence of the mind and of character, has come to be replaced by *preferences* and the *leveraging* of opportunity to get what we want (or think we need).

When we are required to define life as random chaos without order or spiritual/noble purpose, gratification must be instantaneous or it's not gratifying at all. Why wait? Why not just do as you please, and as your senses drive you to consume, right now? Do so immediately, without any thought for tomorrow, let alone next year or the distant future for generations to come, for your business organization, for society. Modern individuals and especially businesses cannot delay desire in the present, even if in so doing, we could take steps to satisfy ourselves better later in time. This is why our budget priorities are ridiculous and our debt is out of control. It is why companies often take extreme risks.

Recent studies show that MBA students leave business school with even less regard for ethical standards than they had upon arrival. They are taught that "dog-eat-dog" survival means there is not really much room for ethics in business. Human judgment, it seems, has been replaced with algorithms. In economic theory, managerial freedom is reduced to zero and no longer viewed positively. Corporate responsibility is considered a cost to be minimized.

Economic theory has reduced human agency to the narrow confines of *homo economicus*, the mythical man who is constantly maximizing profits and never makes decisions that don't hinge on rate of return. For *h. economicus*, there is no long-term thinking, no delayed gratification, no virtuous relationships with the larger society, and certainly no personal sacrifice for the common good. Although this bears no resemblance to how people actually behave, we allow the model to dominate our business decisions. Where there is no leeway for free managerial decision making (since, as we are often told, market forces dictate everything anyhow), there is also no space for the exercise of the virtues that compose common sense.

Economics has lost his way; it used to be closely related to the social and political sciences, but in an effort to become more "scientific," economists pushed values (and with it, real life, since all people hold values) to the outside of their field. Having shifted their field, they were forced to redefine people—as wholly self-interested, always maximizing, and predictable where money is concerned. They lost sight of the common good and replaced it with "aggregate interest."

They lost sight of a healthy society and replaced it with a mass of individuals—who (as many as can) are out to get as much as they can as fast as they can.

Following such economic leads creates a state where managers can't invest in long-term societal good, sustainable practices, or humanistic management (unless they can somehow engineer a short-term profit from it). CEOs with strong convictions are called to abstain from them and follow the path of least resistance, swallowing their ethical angst. After all, their compensation is closely tied to short-term performance, so why shoot yourself in the foot just for an intrinsic value you can't even buy or sell?

This is not to say that economics ought not inform business at all. But it should be centered on the actual human condition. A paradigm shift toward more corporate responsibility is very much in the interest of corporations! The public, in the face of so many calamities, is refusing to wear the *h. economicus* straitjacket and is starting to demand that managers as a matter of course are capable of being held responsible for more than their bottom lines.

Bringing Common Sense Back

We can conclude that any resurrection of the notion of common sense in business will require a rejection of the modernist approach—and this will have profound consequences. Our narrowed perspective has turned prudence into a utility or even worse, some kind of cleverness possessed only by the few and gifted. But it is in fact the virtue *par excellence* for guiding us into an uncertain and ever riskier future. This will demand self-attention but also thoughtful social interaction in our modern setting.

This is because while prudence (an indispensable core of common sense business) may start with the individual, it culminates in our actions together in society. Businesses in particular must implement ethical management as their "core competency" for acting in responsible and humane ways. In this sense, business must in the first instance appeal to common sense and experience—not to some ideology.

As for the economists, they must enter the future with an honest assessment of the professed neutrality of their field. When intrinsic things like faith and spirituality, values, ideas, human life, and aesthetic phenomena are monetized, they are by definition being evaluated and ranked, usually far under financial gain, which holds the highest place. This is far from "neutral," and to insist so is a total illusion.

What we need to achieve is a leap forward into the past, a time when philosophers considered economics part and parcel of the common good, not an adversary to it. Business education, at every level—for MBAs, EMBAs, and executive education—should prepare managers and executives to employ quantitative methods in the service of qualitative evaluations arising from well-reasoned, circumspect, and balanced judgments. And this is too rarely the case at present.

But the winds of change are blowing. Corporations have begun to protect their own longevity by assuring a stable demand for their products rather than by maximizing profits in the shortest term. Others have discovered social entrepreneurship. More than a few have chosen to go down an even more revolutionary, virtuous path—where managers are not viewed as factoids or powerless pawns but rather responsible decision makers. And their decisions always involve qualitative acts of judgment based on common sense for the common good.

In truth, the workings of the economy are not as mysterious as we make them out to be. "The economy" is no more and no less than what "we, the people" do or don't do in terms of business transactions. There is not one rigid set of economic laws that applies everywhere and at all times. Rather, the behavior of individual economic agents changes the "laws" that generalize that very behavior. Hence, there is no other way to find out whether ethical forms of doing business hurt or help the bottom line than to try them out by using plain old common sense. And here then is the good news.

Studies have shown that ethical and patient/sustainable practices do not hurt competitiveness; they have been found to be more than slightly positive.

The possibility for financially viable ethics exists. Consequently, there is a moral responsibility to use it well. Recovering common sense in your business is a leadership journey that builds on competence, grows with authority, is aligned with other virtues, and is grounded on the four Ps of common sense business. The next chapter will explain what we mean.

NOTES

1. *Catechism of the Catholic Church*, section 1806.
2. Ibid., quoting Proverbs 14:15.

PART I:
COMMON-SENSE BUSINESS

CHAPTER 1
WHAT IS COMMON-SENSE BUSINESS?

What it takes to do a job will not be learned from management courses. It is principally a matter of experience, the proper attitude, and common sense—none of which can be taught in a classroom.
—Hyman G. Rickover

Common sense is in spite of, not the result of, education.
—Victor Hugo

Recall from the introduction that we referred to the four Ps of common-sense business. This is our way of simplifying a complex reality. Because of modernism, a lot of the skills, natures, and virtues of common-sense business don't come as naturally as they used to. This book itself is also a simplification of what might end up being very complicated—possibly even a complete overhaul of your firm once you've jumped into common-sense business with both feet.

So we've designed the book to be both deeply informative and immediately useful. To these ends, each part serves an important purpose. Part I expounds upon the four Ps of common sense, as we have developed them (see below). Part II is all about common-sense business around the globe. We include case studies from Norway, Canada, Britain, Japan, India, and Germany—with an in-depth look at a major success story out of Germany. Part III houses some practical tools for you to implement now, advises on how common sense can be applied in the not-for-profit sector, and then ends with some examples of more new companies practicing common-sense business.

The Four Ps of Common-Sense Business

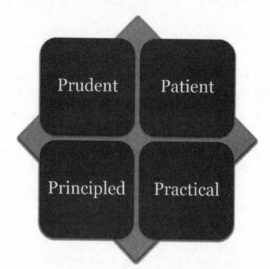

The four Ps of common-sense business are traits that describe the business person who is so desperately needed today: prudent, patient, principled, and practical. You'll see these themes come up a lot in this book, especially in this part I. Chapter 2 is all about prudence, with lessons from an ancient text surprisingly relevant for today. Chapter 3 discusses patience in business through a discussion of patient capital. Chapter 4 is about principled decision making, and chapter 5 gets very practical, with ideas for developing common sense in yourself and others. Chapter 6 introduces what we consider one of the best tools for big-picture planning and decision making: the Virtue Matrix (originally envisioned by Roger L. Martin). Then in chapter 7, we give some real-world examples of common-sense business (or lack of it). We present an example of a major disappointment, a turnaround story, a smart move forward, and a new company addressing an old problem in a brilliant, common-sense way. Chapter 8 goes more in-depth with a classic common-sense company that's withstood the test of time.

Common sense in business is primed for a comeback. It is high time for more practical wisdom and less irrational behavior. This book shows how, why, and where it is being done, and more importantly, how you can do it, too.

CHAPTER 2

LESSONS IN PRUDENCE
FROM ANCIENT WISDOM[1]

The prudent man always studies seriously and earnestly to understand whatever he professes to understand, and not merely to persuade other people that he understands it.

—Adam Smith

With all the talk today of being future-oriented and trend-forward, taking time for reflection on the wisdom of antiquity may seem like a waste of time. But here we make an appeal to the perspective of ancient wisdom as *the original form of common sense.*

In today's modern—or postmodern—world, we can become so jaded that little intrigues us anymore. But those who have enough forethought to look backwards can still actually be amazed at the contemporary relevance of the ancient texts. Whether the common sense is found in the *Analects* of Confucius, the *Analytics* of Aristotle, or the epigrams of the biblical book of Proverbs, it expresses a profound sense of humanity's potential—both good and bad. The words sound old-fashioned, but the truths are timeless; we will always have among us "the sluggard" and "the wicked," as well as "the upright" and "the beneficent."

Written before a time when we were tossed around by every tweet, ancient wisdom texts are rooted in thoughtful observation of practical consequences. They speak to everyday living as well as to community (we could say, corporate and business) life. So what does ancient wisdom from the Bible have to say to us who are looking for firm common-sense footing in our ever-shifting business worlds?

Lessons from Proverbs

Reading Proverbs can be disturbing. Like morning sun after a late night, its 930 sayings can be irritatingly bright. It can also be like the mirror we prefer not to look into first thing in the morning! Here is candor, honesty, and criticism that leaves little room for our excuses. Yes, Proverbs can at times state the obvious and seem to some offensive; more often, it speaks with compelling common sense and invites careful consideration.

You don't have to be a scholar or a person of faith; if you're open to learning, you will find much useful guidance in Proverbs. You might find yourself shaking your head and chuckling, *That is so true.* The wisdom of proverbs ("Wisdom" and "Folly" are represented in the book by competing female characters) says out loud the things we only think to ourselves in the workplace. She has never heard of political correctness. And Folly has never heard of being professionally discreet. But this is one of the injections we need into our current state of disillusionment: a good dose of "whether you want to hear it or not."

Now, Wisdom has no agenda but human flourishing, and she wants the best for you and your business. So let's look at seven classic, common-sense warnings from Proverbs for business and for leaders:

Enmity

Enmity is conflict—and not the polite kind. It is characterized by grudges, clashes, narrowed eyes, and pursed lips. You could call it hatred. And Proverbs doesn't always say that hatred is wrong. "Hatred of evil," for instance, is valued. And even *God* hates: pride, arrogance, corruption, lying, and those who try to break up families.[2] But when it comes to more everyday topics—such as money, power, and personal offenses—Proverbs warns acutely against hatred, because it leads to enmity: "stirring up dissension" and "harsh words" that "stir up anger." So when anger moves from an emotion to a motivating factor for words and action, you're in dangerous territory.

Proverbs has practical advice for us today when we get angry: cool your jets if you don't want to bring down your hangar. By way of contrast, a gentle answer "turns away wrath." Although a hot-headed retort might feel good in the moment, you'll be sorry later: "Fools give vent to all their anger; but the wise, biding their time, control it."[3] Proverbs also warns us that anger can be *caught*; we learn bad habits from having angry friends.

And for goodness' sake, don't go into business with perpetually angry people. If you fall short on your end, Proverbs warns, they'll re-possess your bed right out from under you![4]

How wise of Proverbs to address enmity in everyday life and business. Anger is a fact of life. Speech is a flammable substance. The challenge is to safeguard a space in which to think clearly *and* to consider how to counter anger. Common sense suggests we keep a close eye on those motivated by senseless enmity inside or outside any company.

Misperception

Intentions can be misread, and our own filters can cause us to misjudge what's being said or what's happening. None of us is above this flaw. Proverbs points out a common occurrence that happens in business offices around the world: "The first to present their case seems right, till another comes forward to question it." Also, "A person who lacks judgment derides their neighbor, but a person with understanding holds their tongue"—we could say, keeps his opinions to himself, at least until a more commonsensical time to voice them.[5]

Proverbs is clear that the need to "preserve sound judgment and discernment" is crucial; both must not be allowed "out of your sight." This means that the wise person (or worker, or supervisor, or investor) is never browbeaten into doing what her conscience rejects nor seduced by the allure of money, sex, and power.[6] In the same way, the successful manager neither "provokes" deliberately, nor is easily provoked. As 20:3 states, "It is to a person's honor to avoid strife; every fool is quick to quarrel." The wise don't make snap decisions or misread people or situations. So wisdom warns you that your business is at risk from superficiality and from misperception—whether deliberate or accidental.

Deceit

If "the wisdom of the prudent is to give thought to their ways" in Proverbs 14:8, "the folly of fools is deception." There is a corrosive "deceit in the hearts of those who plot evil." In contrast, a wise, righteous person does not bring a case against another without cause, and she doesn't deliberately lie.

Bringing together the themes of anger, misperception, *and* deceit, Proverbs 26:24–26 warns us to watch out for the employee or partner who can poison a company—sometimes it's the person who is actually the most charismatic. The key is to expose their accusations and enmity to the assessment of a group: "Though their speech is charming, do not believe them. . . . Their malice may be concealed by deception, but their wickedness will be exposed in the assembly."

Of course, this might sound brutally direct and offensive, since we all tell little white lies from time to time. But we shouldn't write off the warning. The key is to be savvy when dealing with those who have proven themselves to be less than truthful. It is better to work with someone who will tell you the hard truth than someone who will sugarcoat a situation in order to keep things comfortable for himself.

You can never afford to assume that data from any party is free of bias or even willful distortion. Whether the information presents a favorable outlook or the threat of meltdown, both reports deserve your careful scrutiny. Because financial and economic power is a powerful drug, addiction to it can lead to some very perverted information coming from certain sources. Before you feed on what they serve you—or are tempted to serve up your own brand of false information—heed Proverbs 20:17: "Food gained by deceit tastes sweet to a person, but they end up with a mouth full of gravel."

Dissent

It sometimes seems similar to straight-talk or telling the hard truth, but dissent is a different animal entirely. Dissent works specifically to divide and conquer. It comes not from a place of honest questioning or challenging but from an attitude of rebellion and superiority.

Proverbs warns about the threat of dissent, because common sense knows that harmony is a priceless treasure. How many companies have we heard about that are torn down from the inside, without a competitor having to raise a finger, because of in-house politics? Disruption of mission, then, must be consciously and carefully avoided. In Proverbs we see this, as the family member who brings "trouble" on his family is warned that he will "inherit only wind." The young are counseled to keep a good head on their shoulders and "not to join with the rebellious." The ruler is urged to sift out the wicked so that his throne is "established through righteousness," and Proverbs 22:10 urges, "Drive out the mocker, and out goes strife; quarrels and insults are ended."[7]

Time and again, Proverbs calls out the schemer, the mocker, the quarrelsome. Do you have employees more interested in drama than in development? In making a personal point than in making group progress? All such people jeopardize social harmony, disturb a group's peace of mind, and threaten to undermine the company mission.

Thankfully, Proverbs also describes ways of making and preserving harmony. A ruler (or boss), we are urged, can be won over by patient kindness, or to put it more colorfully, "a gentle tongue can break a bone."[8] To Proverbs, then, peace is a real possibility, but it is always at risk. Sometimes it requires that we clean house; other times, that we make a kind gesture of acceptance. Finally, common sense suggests that living our own lives free of the folly of dissent will spread peace to those working with us.

Foolishness

Foolishness ("Folly") is seen in the perverse and deliberately contrary, the brash and bombastic, the overly confident and verbally unrestrained. In Proverbs, the raunchy imagery of a prostitute hawking her trade symbolizes how Folly lures her victims.

The fool in Proverbs is "loud," "undisciplined," "hot-headed," and "reckless." Such people "hate knowledge" (so don't try to confuse them with the facts!), "find pleasure in evil conduct," only "trust in themselves," and take "delight in airing their own opinions." The fool's mouth is particularly dangerous. Though ultimately his undoing, in the interim, it tends to incite conflict.[9] To honor this person is likened to "tying a stone in a sling" (it makes no sense and accomplishes nothing). To *hire* such a person, Proverbs warns, is like an archer "shooting at random" (*everyone* gets hurt).[10]

It is the pushy, demanding nature of Folly and her words that Proverbs warns against repeatedly. To some of course, "pushy" behavior might sound acceptable: it expresses personality or enables necessary self-promotion. Certainly no marketing department would be complete without a certain amount of overconfidence; it can be charming, when coupled with an ability to laugh at oneself. But foolishness always takes extraversion to the next level—coercion. Always turns sociable into self-absorbed. The snarky email and the irreverent social-media post are best-beloved pals of these foolish types, who believe that others consciously crave their fine opinions. Contrast this with the discerning who "keep wisdom in view," are "even tempered," "use words with restraint," and are not quick to speak nor easily angered.[11]

Power Hunger

Private anger and willful deceit, dangerous as they are, are frequently dwarfed in the public realm by the abuse of power and the manipulation of position. States Proverbs 28:15–16, "Like a roaring lion or a charging bear is a wicked man ruling over a helpless people. A tyrannical ruler lacks judgment, but the person who hates ill-gotten gain will enjoy a long life." Verse 28 of the same chapter emphasizes the reactions of those supposedly following the so-called leader: "When the wicked rise to power, people go into hiding." Likewise, says Proverbs 29:2, "When the wicked rule, the people groan."

Hunger for power can lead to tyranny, which can poison a company: "By justice a king gives a country stability, but one who is greedy for bribes tears it down." (Consider President Nixon's infamous declaration, "When the President does it, that means that it is not illegal.") And don't think that your foolish greed doesn't spread itself around, because "if a ruler listens to lies, all his officials become wicked."[12]

Laziness

The theme of idleness is prominent in Proverbs. The "sluggard" is criticized as heartily as anyone, so no action at all is considered as detestable as wicked action. The lazy person "turns on his bed" (just five more minutes . . .), avoids hard work and suffers the consequences, protests loudly at imagined threats (like, Proverbs says, a "lion outside the door" blocking his way to work), finds his way "blocked by thorns" (real or imagined, but never his own fault), and still has no doubt that he is wiser than everyone else![13]

In contrast, praise is heaped on the hardworking, prudent, truthful, and diligent,[14] who serve as an example to others. Proverbs 6:6 famously declares its admiration for the hardworking ant: "Go to the ant, you sluggard; consider its ways and be wise!"

The problem with the lazy is not that they just need help getting started; it's that they turn idleness into an end they justify. There is always another reason to take a break, to be excused this time (every time). *Surely someone else will do it.* Behind each excuse lies, we sense, the quest to get "something for nothing." Proverbs solemnly predicts destruction for this person always longing for relief from work: "The sluggard's craving will be the death of him, because his hands refuse to work."[15] The lazy person ruins her body through physical inaction, her mind by twisted rationalization, and her soul by stubborn rebellion.

But this "sluggard" does not suffer alone. His irresponsibility is socially destructive. The lazy are a drain on society. They are, in Proverbs' terms, "brother to one who destroys,"[16] meaning that leaving your own work undone is as bad as tearing down someone else's. Common-sense wisdom in Proverbs and elsewhere unashamedly celebrates work and censures idleness—and so should good, just, and responsible business.

So, ancient wisdom, read as a form of practical common sense, warns businesses of threats from enmity and misperception, from deceit and dissent, from foolishness and tyranny, and lastly, as we have seen, from sheer inactivity. All of these are risks that individuals, firms, and communities always face, to some extent. Wisdom's warnings are worth honoring. Our troubled world doesn't need more troubles; it needs actions and people that are *prudent*. It needs, it begs for common sense. Here is something "better than fine gold and choice silver," Proverbs says about its own wisdom. "With me are riches and honor, wealth that endures, and righteousness."[17]

NOTES

1. This chapter benefits greatly from our dialogue with Christopher D. Hancock, director of Oxford House (which consults on religion, morality, and geopolitics). His ideas on the application of Proverbs to modern life—and the seven common-sense warnings—are integrated here with his permission.

2. Proverbs 6:16–19 and 8:13.

3. Proverbs 28:25, 29:11, 10:12, and 15:1.

4. Proverbs 22:24–27.

5. Proverbs 18:17 and 11:12.
6. Proverbs 3:21, 1:10–19, 5:1–23, and 6:20–7:27.
7. Proverbs 11:29, 24:21, and 25:5.
8. Proverbs 25:15,21 and 16:7.
9. Proverbs 9:13, 14:16, 1:22, 10:23, 28:26, 6:12, 8:13, and 18:2,7,6.
10. Proverbs 26:8,10.
11. Proverbs 17:24,27 and 19:11,19,20.
12. Proverbs 29:4,12
13. Proverbs 10:4, 19:15, 6:9, 26:4, 20:4, 26:13, 15:19, and 26:16.
14. Proverbs 21:5 and 31:27.
15. Proverbs 21:25.
16. Proverbs 18:9.
17. Proverbs 8:35, 3:1–18, and 8:18–19.

CHAPTER 3
PATIENT CAPITAL

Common sense will nearly always stand you in better stead than a slavish adherence to the conventions.

—M.M. Kaye

We made the claim in chapter 1 that common sense is patient. But patience might sound at first to be antithetical to success in business. Believe it or not, when we talk about patience in business, we are shooting for the same "bigger, stronger, faster" that the impatient, flash-in-the-pan businesses are shooting for. And we're after the same worldwide impact and influence. We just want it for the long haul—not only this fiscal quarter. And we want our impact to contribute to the betterment not only of the company but of every group the company touches.

"Patient capital" investing has an eye on long-term stability and strength. It also bridges the gap between the efficiency and scale of market-based approaches and the social impact of pure philanthropy. Patient capital has a high tolerance for risk, masters the long-time horizon, flexes to meet the needs of entrepreneurs, and refuses to sacrifice the needs of end customers for the sake of shareholders. At the same time, patient capital ultimately demands accountability in the form of a healthy return—proof that the underlying enterprise can grow sustainably in the long run. There are boom and bust cycles in any economy, and the U shape demands that companies invest in order to survive. Common sense tells us that such investment requires patient capital, which has a longer-term horizon.

17

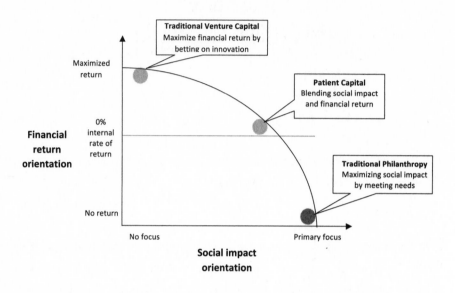

Patient capital isn't just good for people, it's good for profits. There is a palpable impatience infecting much of our investment decision making today, and a corresponding decapitalization of business accompanies it. It's happening in every sector and across industries. As a result, our standard of living as a nation has stagnated, despite an increase of more than 50 percent in economic output since 1970. Real average wages have dropped. There *has* been an increase in productivity (in the 2 percent range), but it is not keeping pace and shows signs of leveling off. Declining prices and swelling competition have left nothing over for wage increases in American business. So most people who feel that their wages in real terms are not going up are right. In recent years, equity has actually flowed *out* of our corporate world. Dividend payments have moved to half of current income, up from less than a quarter only two decades ago. US firms constantly announce stock repurchases (that they probably did not buy at all). The figures are quite astounding. And American companies continue to relocate overseas because of taxes, transfer pricing, or holidays offered by distant regimes.

American Impatience

Asian and European companies, which follow systems defined by dedicated and patient capital, are outperforming US businesses in general. And they invest in both tangible and intangible assets at a noticeably higher rate. Business owners in these locales consider themselves principals rather than agents, so they seek long-term appreciation for shares, which are generally held by buyers for long periods of time. US publicly traded companies, by contrast, increasingly chase the approval of the transitory owner. The stockholders themselves are indoctrinated to buy low and sell high—and quickly. It's part of the rush of "playing" the market. In order to feed the need of the impatient stockholder, firms favor consumption and debt over earnings and capital formation—whatever will post the right numbers. Spending a fiscal quarter investing in assets would result in a knee-jerk reaction by stockholders to the resulting short-term decline in profits.

So despite growth in many sectors, shareholders are not benefiting. If you compare US shareholder earnings over the past thirty years with those for Asian and European counterparts (and adjust for currency fluctuations and purchasing power), the US shareholder has not done so well.

Challenges to Patient Capital

Europe may have a stagnation problem in terms of jobs and employment rigidities, but they are still building plants, training their workforce, and developing new products. As for Asian companies, they are expanding in every possible way. Why are firms in the United States behaving differently? There are four things to consider:

Over the past fifty years, US companies have concentrated on the need to improve their return on investment and earnings per share. This was easy to do by decreasing the size of the denominator—cut the asset size down and keep the earnings the same. This results in an increased ROI. Then if you buy your stock back, you further increase your earnings per share. Like most of America, management are influenced by their own compensation, which is based on current accounting profits, or by unrestricted stock options that heighten stock price sensitivity.

Business schools have done a very good job of turning out bright people who have figured out how to do this denominator magic and do it efficiently. Underinvest in intangible assets, and improve return on investment. That's why net investment in fixed assets has fallen from twenty-five years ago. Important intangible assets such as research, workforce development, and establishing brand names, new products, new markets, and first-rate distribution systems are all underfunded. Meanwhile, US industry continues to spend on acquisitions. Much of the "investment" in acquisitions is only a change in ownership. It does not create anything new. If you build a steel mill in Arizona, for instance, you take a big hit. The start-up costs can kill you. Acquiring a mill, on the other hand, means smoother sailing for now—though it also means less innovation, job creation, and improvement from the ground up.

US companies also demand higher hurdle rates than do their foreign competitors; we won't invest unless we can expect a return of more than 12 percent. That's the "cost of money" in our minds. If you look at the ROIs of Asian, European, and US companies, you will find US companies outperforming the other two by about five percentage points. But the higher hurdle rate in the United States only gives Asian and European companies a performance umbrella to work under while dissuading US firms from making a whole range of important investments.

The third reason is that the real owners of US business today are retirement funds. Fifty years ago, 70 percent of stock ownership was in private hands. Today more than 70 percent is in the hands of pension and mutual funds. We have passed the responsibility for managing on to an agent, and this is essentially incompatible with capitalism. Capitalism in the long run relies on people and their interaction with businesses. When we lose that because our economy is based mostly on institutional and not individual investors, we lose a core strength. Individuals think about long-term gain. Most of our agents trade not only quarterly but nowadays by the nanosecond.

In an ideal world, the process of capital investment in a nation would align itself with returns of private investors and those of society overall. But our brokers are making all the decisions for us, and their goals are chiefly to keep their clients happy by fattening their portfolios. While the US capital system is still the most effective, it is not *because* it creates a divergence of interests between shareholders and corporations; it is in spite of that. The US system in fact impedes the flow of capital to those corporate investments with the greatest social and private payoffs over the long-term.

Finally, the current governance system of US companies does not serve the companies well. Bankers, customers, or suppliers can't serve as members of a company's board of directors. But the Asians and Europeans don't face the same laws and take full advantage of their insight. Further, we have laws that keep shareholding in the United States fragmented rather than concentrated. The power of group influence to inform companies for the better is therefore diluted. Management has to interpret signals from somewhere, and their views are frequently colored by the latest televised sound bite. Corporate boards have become dominated by outside directors with no other links to the company, and they exert only a limited influence on corporate decision making anyway.

What's more, the agent who now does the investing for us does not have a tax consequence when he makes a trade. So pension funds will sell a company out on a whim or a rumor and will manipulate the last decimal point, any time day or night. The rest of us have a 40 percent cost on selling stock.

Investing with Common Sense

In light of these challenges, how can we in the United States still practice patient capital and invest with common sense? First, we must not fear failure in the short-term, even though stockholders may balk. This is easier said than done; we are a society that punishes failure. But making some investments that fail is essential to a dynamic plan of learning and growth. An institutional structure that overpenalizes failed investments may in fact, over time, undermine the competitive capacity of a firm.

Some investments generate no profit but rather create capabilities that benefit future development. Certainly, a company can increase profits by cutting out certain things—such as R&D, employee training, and customer relations. However, you would also "save" yourself the trouble of invaluable social returns such as watching candidates compete to work for you, seeing worker skills grow, and improved quality of your product and service. You also wouldn't have to worry about happy customers and cutting-edge breakthroughs that raise your firm's leadership in the field.

Policies to Encourage Patient Capital

Governance in most US publicly traded companies is not for perpetuation or long-term investment and strategy. To curtail this trend and stop decapitalization, we should tax pension funds so they have a transaction cost. If they hold a stock for less than one year, they should be taxed at forty percent and let the rate decrease annually so that in year five, there would be no tax on trades. Only then would pension funds look at companies that had some kind of long-term future.

This kind of proposal would have lots of advantages: it would increase government revenues, correct the tax inequity between individuals and institutions, punish short-term stock speculation strategies, and focus ownership on long-term performance. It would also give management courage to stop playing the game of "denominator management." It is likely that transaction costs would also drop, because there would be less churning, thereby increasing investment in the US economy. This could improve the savings rate, increase jobs, and help to get the capital gains tax down for transactions within a family or closely held unit.

We should also relax some restrictions and allow banks to hold stock in companies and bank directors to sit on boards. They are allowed to do so in Germany and Japan.

These changes would start to align the firm with the purpose of society—and that is a profound task in front of business everywhere. We need to invest in those intangible items— training the labor force, new distribution systems, and research and development—for the very future of business. If we fail to do so, we are going to end up in the near future seeing the last public company in the United States disappear.

CHAPTER 4

THE ADDICTIVE LURE
OF FINANCIAL DOPING

Common sense is seeing things as they are; and doing things as they ought to be.

—Harriet Beecher Stowe

"Principled" is one of the four Ps of common-sense business. We would go so far as to say that no business can survive for long (or thrive at all) without principles. But principles don't show up on the P&L statement. They are deep seated and hard to describe. In today's world, they are sometimes even hard to admit to. To have a principle means to believe that something is right and good and another thing is wrong and bad. Heaven forbid we take a stand on anything. We are much more comfortable with what we would call "synthetic business." Something synthetic, as defined by Merriam Webster, is "devised, arranged, or fabricated for special situations to imitate or replace usual realities." On the surface, modern-day investment bankers, traders, and baseball and other sports superstars might not seem to have very much in common. But all have been caught dealing in synthetics.

Recently the *Financial Times* reported that two of the largest banks in the country (if not the world), Morgan Stanley and J.P. Morgan, were looking to relaunch the giant boom-or-bust synthetic CDOs[1] that nearly doomed the world economy and caused the painful crash of 2008. These two giant banks are not alone. *Bloomberg* reported that Citigroup had already sold one billion dollars in CDO products only a few months into the calendar year. Now, the global economy lost some thirty-five *trillion* dollars in assets from that financial crisis, and it has yet to fully recover. Was anything learned from the experience?

With corporate bond yield rates dropping, banks are growing increasingly frustrated. The need for "fast money" again is luring banks into devising, selling, and marketing these same old spineless synthetic financial products, the very ones that caused the crisis. The new push for synthetics is driven by investors that are aggressively seeking high-yield investments in securities outside of the flat corporate bond market. This thirst for rapid profit among banks and investors alike has created what could be called a modern day financial doping (synthetics) scandal. Like addicts, we can't seem to "just say no"—or get clean from the drugs.

This is a societal problem. Despite the warnings and tremendous risk, baseball and other sports players are still turning to doping and synthetic means to enhance athletic performance. Alex Rodriguez, the fastest player in the history of baseball to hit six hundred home runs, was finally forced to admit to substance use, and that has literally ended his career. "A-Rod" was once one of the awe-inspiring talents of the game. Now his career has come crashing down à la Bear Stearns and Lehman Brothers. He is like cyclist Lance Armstrong, a liar and a cheat, and he will be stripped of his honors. He has to wait until December 2021 to find out, but no one is predicting he will enter the Hall of Fame—rather, the Hall of Shame.

The Rush and the Crash

Drug-like addictions to short-term booming success, whether in home runs or in derivatives, has led to the destruction of century-old companies, of the careers of iconic figures, and of the reputation of both the financial professional and America's favorite pastime. And the trend is global, as we saw among the international community of the most recent Olympics.

These collapses, scandals, and crimes demonstrate an ethical decay never seen before in our history. Societal addiction to synthetics penetrates so deeply that investors and sport fans both now have more or less come to expect scandal rather than old-fashioned success. But don't we remember from our Halloween-candy gorges of childhood that with the (sugar) rush always comes the crash? To the six-year-old, understandably, the trade-off is worth it. But it appears we haven't all outgrown our tendency to overindulge in "junk food." Today, the risk of financial, societal, or career crash is accepted over prudent behavior fashioned by common sense.

Occasional losses are part and parcel of a capitalist economy and of everyday existence. Life is full of ups and downs, and no one is great every day. No matter how much quantitative acumen a trader might have, no Wall Street "all star" can consistently and perpetually hit the ball over the fence for investors and shareholders. Just ask Buddy Fox. Even the infamous Wolf of Wall Street—depicted in the movie by that name—got caught. Incredibly, in 2012, there were eight high-profile financial scandals in a period of only five months. The year after that, there were thirty more, and the list keeps growing and growing.

We appear to have learned next to nothing from the past. Firms and sports players alike have not only shifted or lost their sense of judgment, but have dramatically lost their way. The entire landscape has radically changed. Companies and employees may know right from wrong and may have an ethical compass, but they are lured by the fame that comes from fast money—not to speak of the lucrative economic and psychic rewards.

What has happened to selling products where you actually have "skin in the game"? What happened to hard work, reputation, and devotion? Are these common-sense notions lost? Most frustratingly, there is little push to change the current system, whether in the form of regulation, character development, or independent governance.

Short-Termism: Our Economic Vice

A stubborn addiction to short-termism is at the very root of the problem, and admittedly, no regulation can fix it. It is both a mania and a mantra. Financial icons and athletes alike focus on results *now*, and to hell with the consequences and any lingering ethical qualms. They are willing to sacrifice long-term reputation and profitability for a quick hit.

The change from previous generations is dramatic. Bygone baseball stars like Babe Ruth, Hank Aaron, Willie Mays, and Mickey Mantle all became icons through talent and hard work—*lots* of hard work—and sacrifice. The same was true in the privately held firms of yesteryear and in capital markets where careers were earned and promotions made over many decades, not months. The partners in a firm put their own money and reputations on the line as a cost of doing business. They did have lots of skin in the game.

To move forward, our moral fabric and way of doing business must fundamentally change. The current race to the bottom in sports and in finance is surely not sustainable or prudent; it has lost any idea of common sense. Realities of universal limitations must be accepted. Out of control, "high-yield" greed must be rejected. The effects of PEDs on our way of life as well as our financial system are telltale. Synthetic cowardice can make anyone a fifteen-minute superstar, yet fifteen minutes hardly lasts forever. It is not sustainable.

The Road to Rehab

Unless we restrict the use of financial PEDs, the entire system is likely to spin out of control (again). And the way to curtail such behavior was outlined in the second part of *The End of Ethics and a Way Back*,[2] where we talked about "A Way Back." That hard way back is paved along three necessary axes. The first is *personal responsibility* based in character. Ethical people are not born; they are nurtured and trained in the habits of doing what is right and of appreciating the good while resisting the bad and the wrong. Next, these people—when joined together in social units, and especially in forming or joining corporations—can envision and build sustainable *cultures of integrity*. It can be done; many companies across all industries, in every country and tradition, and of every size are living proof.[3]

Ethical, prudent leadership is so critical; the tone at the top matters. That is why the final piece of any return to common sense is necessarily *regulatory regimes*. Now, we don't start there, and we do not believe that ethics or prudence can be fully legislated. However, it is increasingly clear that in various countries, and especially across international boundaries, some regulation (not mere compliance or box ticking) is required to guide—and even at times direct—companies to do the right thing. This includes everything from corporate governance to foreign bribery to enterprise-wide risk management to sustainability measures. (While we all wait for such common-sense legislation, you can get started with the tools provided in part III of this book.)

Overcoming our present predicament will require nothing short of a transformation—and that change is best carried out by remembering the virtue and practice of principles rooted in common sense. Any short-termism that pursues one's own benefits at the expense of everyone else's interests will, sooner rather than later, bring down the house. In short, egotistic action is not in one's informed self-interest. The principled businessperson will want to succeed not only today but also tomorrow. Hence, using common-sense business, we must be rooted enough in our principles to resist the pull of financial doping.

NOTES

1. Synthetic CDOs (collateralized debt obligations) are risky ventures that rely on another's *default* for the meeting of their own investment goals.
2. Theodore Roosevelt Malloch and Jordan D. Mamorsky, *The End of Ethics and A Way Back: How to Fix a Fundamentally Broken Global Financial System* (Wiley, 2013).
3. See Theodore Roosevelt Malloch, *Doing Virtuous Business: The Remarkable Success of Spiritual Enterprise* (Thomas Nelson, 2008).

CHAPTER 5

PRACTICAL SKILLS FOR COMMON-SENSE BUSINESS

The three great essentials to achieve anything worthwhile are, first, hard work; second, stick-to-itiveness; third, common sense.
—Thomas A. Edison

Common sense is called "common" for a reason. You're either born with it, or you're born with it. It is an innate ability, found in all persons to varying degrees, so there's no hopeless case (though given our current state, one might wonder).

It is good news for all of us that common sense can be nurtured and developed, honed and refined. But as a form of native intelligence, it must be practiced in order to maintain its qualities. If you don't employ common sense, it can dwindle over time and is then all the harder to regain. Our best hope is to practice the elements of common sense business until they become habits and then hold ourselves accountable to common sense thinking through regular audits and evaluations (see more about audits in chapter 12).

There are, we think, fifteen elements that go into common-sense business thinking. Working on all of the elements is necessary and in some sense also never fully complete. Common sense should be considered a work in progress as well as a skill base. A program to develop each element and then combine them together will make any leader—indeed any person—more commonsensical in business or in any other domain. We define each element below and give some suggestions that will help you refine your own common sense. Combined, the whole list of elements makes for consistent and comprehensive acumen that can organically revolutionize how business is done at every level of a firm.

1. Sense-making is a cognitive edge to deal with the ambiguity that surrounds us. It creates awareness and understanding in situations of complexity and uncertainty so that managers can execute sound decisions. Sense-making requires a calm perspective on a situation that transcends time and space and lasts beyond the specific moment. Does chaos overwhelm you, or do you see it as an opportunity to gather information, sort out priorities, and act on what's happening?

Nurturing sense-making: In the midst of chaos, practice the four Ps of common sense (see chapter 1). To be ready when the chaos comes, stay one step ahead of it. Consider a multidisciplinary "Futures Thinking" methodology for strategic planning, proximity approaches to marketing and management, and theories or strategies that anticipate and plan around hard decisions.

2. Wisdom is composed of knowledge (what's really happening), discernment (why it's happening), and good judgment (what we can do about it). It leads to an optimism that holds that problems can be solved and to a sense of calm in hard circumstances. By seeing the bigger picture, a wise person or leader can maintain (and offer to others) a sense of proportion and introspection. Wisdom focuses on purpose, not immediate gratification or pleasure. It should strengthen with time and experience.

Nurturing wisdom: Examples include challenging the status quo, balancing self-interest and the common good, and trying to understand without judging.

3. Observation is the action and process of closely viewing or monitoring a thing or person(s). Think about the astronomer who gazes for a lifetime into interstellar galaxies and so is first to notice the new star that crops up unannounced. Or the bank teller who just knows that *some*thing isn't right about the counterfeit bill she receives.

Nurturing observation: Actively acquire information by employing all the senses. Think about processes scientifically: what can you observe is happening? How do plans on paper translate into observable actions on the real sales floor, the staff meeting, the end-user experience? Use the collected data as the basis for discovery.

4. Memorization is simply learning something so well that you can remember it exactly. Some important elements of your business must be able to roll off your tongue as easily as your own birth date. Actors memorize their lines, and the constant repetition helps them to actually become the character.

Nurturing memorization: You will never reach your maximum memorization potential, so start now. Practice with inspiring poems or a verse from scripture. Memorize your mission statement, your employee's names and positions, and accurate and sincere responses to difficult questions. Quote important facts and goals in conversations with those who need to be on board with the mission.

5. Curiosity means an eagerness to know and learn. It arouses the area of the brain that is excitable, speculative, and centers on the unusual, odd, or inexplicable. The scientists landing the Mars Rover were especially curious about the surface they knew little about. That's why they didn't just stop at the moon.

Nurturing curiosity: Value outside-the-box thinking in yourself and others. Listen to the excitement that wells up, and follow its lead to new frontiers. Always ask the questions that come to mind when receiving information, whether out loud to the giver of the information or within yourself for later investigation. Once you've mapped the moon, move on to Mars.

6. Creativity is a phenomenon whereby something new and valuable is formed. This can be a physical object or an intangible idea. Innovation as a result of creativity (such as labor-saving devices and medical advances) allows us to move ahead in better ways. Creativity can be exercised in areas as divergent as artistic expression and analytical calculus.

Nurturing creativity: Conduct conducive environments. Ask "What would happen if . . . ?" Collaborate. Seek out serendipitous opportunities. Pursue a spiritual muse, an artistic outlet, and imaginative thinking.

7. Focus is a cognitive process selectively concentrating on one aspect of the environment while ignoring all others. In science, focus has to do with computations. In optics, it is the image point where light rays originate. As a method of sense-making, focus can be achieved through deep investigation of a defined subject or single problem.

Nurturing focus: Practice keeping focus on the task, problem, or person at hand. Listen for and resist attempts (from outside or inside yourself) to divert focus. Break up large tasks into smaller areas that can be focused on individually.

8. Verbalization is the act of saying something out loud. As the spoken expression of humans, it allows for the emoting of feelings and the decoding of thoughts and images. This translation of interior imagery to transmittable content to verbal expression promotes higher-level thought as well as critical-thinking skills.

Nurturing verbalization: Recognize that all words are translations of thoughts, feelings, and images. Practice speaking out complex ideas in ways that different types of listeners can grasp. Give small-group speeches regularly and receive feedback from listeners. Experiment with verbalizing more slowly, more quickly, more freely, more cautiously, etc.

9. Spatial ability is the awareness of oneself in space. This organizational knowledge of objects in relation to self in a given space provides for alignment and positioning. It makes understanding of the relationship of and between objects knowable in changing circumstances and placements. Think about space, however, as more than measurable airspace; it is also about context, points on a timeline, and placement in a pecking order.

Nurturing spatial ability: Keep maps in your head concerning a variety of zones and capacities: geography, cartography, culture. What is your position in your company? Not just your job title, but your *position?* Who is above, below, beside you? How does your company fit culturally, economically, and geographically within the worlds it inhabits?

10. Social skills are any skills that facilitate interaction and communication with others. These rules and relations are communicated in both verbal and nonverbal forms. The process of learning this set of skills is called socialization.

Nurturing social skills: Seek out admirable mentors. Note the thoughts and feelings that you send to others both verbally and nonverbally. Connect with others in ways that express empathy, healthy self-disclosure, and respectful contact. Avoid the enemies of socialization: arrogance, prejudice, insecurity, and ignorance.

11. Cleverness is an ability to understand and know quickly and easily. This intelligence by design is characterized by brightness and mental agility. By exhibiting ingenuity or imagination in an artful way, one is found to be clever or even shrewd. Charles Darwin was particularly considered clever by his peers for his findings on evolutionary dynamics.

Nurturing cleverness: Put yourself in problem-solving situations, both real and imagined. Practice finding solutions with varied amounts and types of resources. Think about a current system in your firm, and imagine it without one of its important elements. How could you find a clever replacement to the element?

12. Organization is the practice of bringing multiple people, institutions, associations, or groups together to achieve a common goal. Organization comes in many sizes, types, structures, and ecologies—both formal and informal. Leadership is the authority position in organization. Mission is the task of organization.

Nurturing organization: Observe commonalities about the people and things surrounding you that group them into categories. Imagine how the different categories could work together in useful ways. Practice jumping quickly among different perspectives shared by various groups. Imagine how mission could be simultaneously achieved at distant levels of organization.

13. Complexity reduction helps people and organizations simplify strategy, products, processes, and information technology. More complication negatively affects operating models, leading to slow growth, bureaucratization, higher costs, and poorer returns. On a personnel level, complexity leads to frustration and demoralization. Streamlining allows for more direct decision making to serve better both core customers and employees.

Nurturing complexity reduction: Budget for the cause of complexity reduction. Use observation to discover complexity. Consider implementing an evaluation of current systems, looking for redundancies (repeated efforts in multiple departments) as well as outdated efforts that only solve old problems. Invest in nontangible but effective solutions such as training in techniques and the outsourcing or insourcing of processes.

14. Intuition is the ability to understand a thing instinctively, without the need for conscious reasoning. Such insight, inklings, or hunches allow for direct perception of truth or fact, independent of verification processes or immediate apprehension. Founded out of past experiences, these "gut feelings" are not magic but based in past, deep knowledge and memory. It is closely akin to wisdom, observation, and focus.

Nurturing intuition: Look for patterns in situations. While avoiding generalization and prejudices, strive to learn from each experience—both successes and failures. Compare first reactions to final evaluations. How right were your early premonitions? If you are normally slow and careful, force yourself to make snap decisions on occasion based on gut-level feelings.

15. Inspiration is the desire to do something that is worthwhile. It can also be the force or influence that inspires action. People, places, and experiences all can inspire. Personal stories, religion, art, film, literature, music, and dramatic speeches are all potential sources of inspiration.

Nurturing inspiration: Discover the inspiration behind your business's mission. What sparked the flame however long ago? Consider your own inspirations for actions. Seek out those experiences, places, and people who energize you to greatness. Using the skills of memorization and focus, keep inspiration always before you. Strive to inspire others.

The Virtue Matrix

Anyone who's ever built anything knows that skills and talents are only half the story. Tools are needed to get the job done. That's why we've included part III of this book. But we've put one of our favorite and most ingenious tools, the Virtue Matrix, here in the next chapter. Created by a respected friend Roger Martin, it's the most useful tool we've discovered for applying the *prudence, patience,* and *principles* of common-sense business in an exceptionally *practical* way. So while you're nurturing the fifteen elements of common sense in your personal and business life, you can begin applying them through the Virtue Matrix.

CHAPTER 6

THE VIRTUE MATRIX[1]

I think we do ourselves a disservice when we don't really have the pride in our potential and the impact that we can have. And I think the more we can be clear about what we're doing and why we're doing it . . . the more respected business will ultimately be.

—Michael Porter, Harvard Business School[2]

Corporations don't operate in a universe composed solely of share-holders. They exist within larger political and social entities and are subject to pressures from members of those networks, be they citizens concerned about environmental pollution, employees seeking to strike a balance between work and family, or political authorities protective of their tax bases. When the interests of shareholders and the larger community collide, management typically—and quite rationally—sides with shareholders. The almost inevitable next step is for management to come under fire for favoring the narrow interests of shareholders over the broader interests of the community.

The interests of shareholders and those of the larger community are not always opposed, of course. Corporations often willingly engage in socially responsible behavior precisely because it enhances shareholder value. They choose to undertake philanthropic activities such as supporting local museums or soup kitchens because they believe such activities create goodwill among customers in excess of their price tag. Likewise, companies provide daycare and exercise facilities because the improved productivity and retention rates generated by these perks outweigh their cost. And a growing number of companies such as The Body Shop, a global skin- and hair-care retailer, make corporate virtue part of their value proposition: buy one of our products, they tell customers, and you improve the lives of women in developing countries, promote animal rights, protect the environment, and otherwise increase the supply of social responsibility.

There's a second class of socially responsible corporate conduct that generates shareholder value by keeping a business on the right side of the law. For example, company compliance with worker-safety regulations and sexual-harassment statutes serves shareholders' interests by keeping a company free from legal sanctions and safeguarding its reputation.

Clearly, then, shareholder value and social responsibility are not necessarily incompatible. Whether their activities are dictated by choice—supporting charities and cultural institutions, for instance—or by compliance to laws and regulations, corporations can and do serve shareholders' interests while also serving those of the larger community. Such forms of corporate social responsibility could be called *instrumental*. That is, they explicitly serve the purpose of enhancing shareholder value. When it comes to our current supply of responsible corporate behavior, instrumental practices make up the bulk. If the corporate consensus is that a particular activity will *not* accrue to shareholders' benefit, no one corporation is likely to take the initiative to disprove that assumption. Thus, executives' commendable concern for their shareholders' wealth can sometimes stifle innovations in corporate social responsibility.

Another set of activities, however, serves the interests of the larger community but is not guaranteed to do the same for shareholder value. In fact, these activities may diminish it. The motivation for such activities is not instrumental—that is, impelled by the clear purpose of enhancing shareholder value—but *intrinsic*: A company's leaders embark on a course of action simply because they think it's the right thing to do, whether or not shareholder interests are served.

Some intrinsically motivated actions turn out to benefit shareholders as well as society. Henry Ford believed he ought to pay his workers enough to afford to buy the cars they produced. That policy appeared to place him at a disadvantage, since the wages and job security at his plants were well in excess of the norms in the auto industry at the time. But his decision ultimately benefited Ford Motor Company by making it an attractive employer and by stimulating demand for its products. At the same time, Ford's move benefited society in the long term by raising the bar for pay and labor practices across the auto industry.

Other intrinsic activities, like the renowned Malden Mills case, benefit society at the shareholders' expense: a 1995 fire destroyed a textile plant in northern Massachusetts, and owner Aaron Feuerstein used his $300 million insurance settlement to not only rebuild the plant but also pay his workers while it was under construction. Finally, some intrinsic actions, unless widely adopted, are both detrimental to shareholders and ineffectual in establishing socially beneficial norms. For instance, the leaders of a chemical producer may believe that investing heavily in greenhouse-gas reduction is the right thing to do. But if the producer's rivals refuse to follow suit, the company may undermine its own cost-competitiveness without significantly lowering overall greenhouse-gas emissions.

The Virtue Matrix Tool

Executives are under increasing pressure to ensure that the companies they lead are "good"—which variously means ethical, responsible, sustainable, environmentally friendly, and respectful of laws, regulations, and international codes of conduct. They also are expected to honor the investment of their shareholders and win earnings for them. In short, they have to be model citizens but also financial celebrities. In the midst of all this pressure, what's a CEO to do? How does a leadership team learn about and then make sound decisions about the ever-broadening range of societal issues and all the interests they face?

In retrospect, of course, it is fairly easy to determine whether a particular corporate action benefited shareholders, society, both, or neither. But corporate leaders don't believe in hindsight when making their decisions. They can, however, use the Virtue Matrix as a framework for assessing opportunities for socially responsible behavior. In this way, prudent use of the matrix nurtures both sense-making and wisdom (the first two practical skills of common-sense business; see chapter 5). The ultimate purpose of the matrix is to offer a set of decisions and commitments that are achievable, tenable, defensible, affordable, and even profitable. Done properly and executed well, they can result in a company gaining strength, living longer, and generating more value as a result in a company. That is the very definition of responsibility. The tool helps CEOs understand and make decisions—hard choices—about what a company should do to ensure that it is managing risks as well as appropriately exploring and leveraging opportunities.

By offering the Virtue Matrix, we are not suggesting that you throw out everything that you know and do in order to make new corporate citizenship decisions from the ground up. We recognize that there are countless ways for companies to create value. What is needed is a tool that allows companies to develop and choose the options that are best fitted to each company. Many of the systems for corporate citizenship may already be in place to one degree or another. But a consistent corporate-citizenship strategy may still be lacking. It takes time, knowledge, and tools like the Virtue Matrix to create one.

The matrix is composed of four quadrants. The bottom two make up the "foundation" of the matrix; the top two are its "frontier." The lower two quadrants are what can be called the civil foundation. Akin to the "common law" of responsible corporate behavior, the civil foundation is an accumulation of customs, norms, laws, and regulations. It promotes conduct that is socially responsible *and* enhances shareholder value.

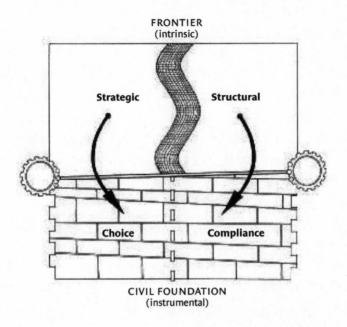

FRONTIER
(intrinsic)

Strategic   Structural

Choice   Compliance

CIVIL FOUNDATION
(instrumental)

In the lower left quadrant resides conduct that corporations engage in by choice, in accordance with norms and customs. The lower right quadrant represents compliance—responsible conduct mandated by law or regulation. A dotted line divides the choice side of the civil foundation from the compliance side, indicating that the boundary between the two is porous.

Perhaps the most significant aspect of the civil foundation is its upper limit—that is, the line separating it from the frontier quadrants. It is not fixed but rather mounted on two gears that can raise or lower the bar. In robust economies, the limiting line tends to move upward over time, as new social benefits become norms or even legal requirements. But the civil foundation can shrink as well as expand. Pressures on less-healthy economies can weaken the norms—and in some cases, even the legal enforcement—that support the civil foundation.

For a case in point, consider Russia immediately following the collapse of Soviet rule: regulations governing working conditions, child labor, and the like were largely not enforced, and legal authorities—far from protecting state assets—participated in their wholesale looting. As a result, commercial enterprises, which had been subject to at least minimal discipline by Soviet authorities, became vehicles for the enrichment of a handful of plutocrats. Only in the past few years, as foreign financiers have conditioned their investments on a modicum of responsible corporate behavior, has Russia reestablished the semblance of a civil foundation.

The top two quadrants of the matrix, the strategic and structural frontiers, encompass activities whose motivation tends to be intrinsic and whose value to shareholders is either clearly negative or not immediately apparent. The strategic frontier includes activities that may add to shareholder value—and become instrumental—by generating positive reactions from customers, employees, or legal authorities. Actions that fit in this quadrant, though risky, are nonetheless generated by the conscious choice of the corporation's senior management as part of their profit-making strategy.

Socially responsible corporate practices in the strategic frontier tend to migrate to the civil foundation as other companies imitate the innovator until the practice becomes the norm. An example is Prudential Insurance's 1990 introduction of viatical settlements— contracts that allow people with AIDS, for instance, to tap into the death benefits in their life insurance policies to pay for current medical and related expenses. The move generated so much goodwill that competing insurers soon began offering this as well. Very quickly, corporate behavior that had seemed radical became business as usual throughout the insurance industry.

The upper right quadrant of the matrix, the structural frontier, houses activities that are both intrinsically motivated and turn out to be contrary to the interests of shareholders. The benefits of corporate conduct in this quadrant accrue principally to society rather than to the corporation, creating a fundamental structural barrier to corporate action. The Malden Mills example is a classic case of conduct on the structural frontier. By continuing to pay his employees, the mill's owner spared them considerable hardship and relieved the state and city of the costs of unemployment insurance and welfare payments. But his generous act decreased his own wealth and that of his fellow shareholders. Unlike Prudential's actions, Aaron Feuerstein's conduct will probably not become the norm in corporate America.

The strategic and structural frontiers are separated by a wavy line, which is intended to suggest that some actions are not *clearly* beneficial or detrimental to shareholders, so placing them in a distinct quadrant is difficult. For instance, Procter & Gamble had a strict policy of refusing to pay bribes to win foreign business long before the Foreign Corrupt Practices Act banned such conduct. While this may have placed the company at a disadvantage compared to its rivals, P&G's improved reputation among consumers in the United States and elsewhere likely offset that harm. On the whole, though, actions that fall between the strategic and structural frontiers tend to gravitate, by default, toward the structural.

Some activities that enter the civil foundation through the left quadrant eventually become so widespread that the norms are enshrined in laws or regulations and take up residence in the right quadrant. Hence the dividing line between the two is dotted and can be crossed. For example, only a handful of companies once offered health-care benefits to employees' dependents. Because the goodwill engendered among employees and customers exceeded the cost of the benefits, more companies copied the practice. Eventually, government regulations required most companies offering health benefits to employees to extend them to dependents as well.

Having toured the Virtue Matrix, let's use it to analyze the issues confronting senior executives when they consider their corporations' social responsibilities. The first one to tackle is why the public clamor for more responsible corporate conduct never seems to abate.

No Good Deed Goes Unpunished

Some companies are near-paragons of socially responsible behavior. They support worthy causes in their communities, their workforces are diverse, their policies are family-friendly. They go well beyond the minimum safeguards required by environmental regulations. Yet many citizens, interest groups, and media commentators complain that these very companies are insufficiently attentive to the common good. What explains the public's perception that, at any given time, there is an undersupply of corporate social responsibility?

In a sense, companies are victims of their own good deeds. Consider again the civil foundation of the Virtue Matrix. Corporate behavior that falls into the lower quadrants may have originated on the strategic frontier, but today it is either mandated by law or enforced by custom and tradition. Thus complying with environmental law or providing onsite day care now wins corporations little credit in the public mind, even if a firm had been previously at the forefront of provision of such services.

For a company to earn public credit for its behavior, it has to engage in activities that *currently* reside in the frontier. This is where the public perceives obvious social or environmental benefits to be gained but little corporate willingness to realize them. But at any given time, only a few companies are operating on the strategic frontier.

The picture is even worse on the structural frontier. The fresh establishment of admirable industry-wide policies is so tricky that it's nearly always a bust. Consequently, no consortium of energy producers has come together to formulate and execute a strategy to reduce greenhouse-gas emissions. Pharmaceutical manufacturers have not yet crafted a plan to halt the worldwide spread of HIV infection. Media companies have failed to take concerted action to stem the tide of vulgar trash that too often passes for children's entertainment. There are compelling commercial, scientific, and political reasons why these initiatives have not come to pass, but the inability or unwillingness to deliver these obvious benefits creates a powerful public sense that corporations are not doing enough.

The Vision Shortage

The most significant impediment to the growth of corporate virtue is a dearth of vision among business leaders. Opportunities abound to devise programs and processes that benefit society as they enrich shareholders. What seems lacking is imagination and intrinsic motivation on the part of corporations and executives. This is by no means an insurmountable obstacle. Fundamental economics are on the side of innovation in the strategic frontier. What's needed is support for the companies and business leaders who undertake bold initiatives. This support is essential, since the benefits of innovation on the strategic frontier are speculative until action is taken.

Consumer agitation can help executives weigh the risks of action. For example, Scandinavian consumers have long pressed for more environmentally friendly paper products, such as toilet tissue and disposable diapers. This pressure helped convince Scandinavian paper producers to take a chance on innovations such as using unbleached pulp in their products.

Perhaps even more effective than consumer agitation is peer encouragement. By publicizing their successes won on the strategic frontier, business leaders can encourage further innovation by other companies. Prudential made a point of trumpeting the enthusiastic market acceptance of viatical settlements. Favorable newspaper articles and TV spots about the settlements convinced rival insurers that the risk of introducing similar products was negligible compared with the potential benefits.

Far more troublesome and difficult to dislodge are barriers to action on the structural frontier. (As a result, the solutions we propose are provisional, and we encourage readers to challenge and extend my thinking on this question.) The greatest barrier here is the lack of economic incentives. Agitation from consumers won't sway companies here, since, by definition, if consumers were enthusiastic enough to likely reward corporations for a particular innovation, that innovation would be located on the strategic frontier. Nonetheless, there are ways to overcome this bias toward the status quo. The most effective weapon against inertia is collective action, either on the part of governments, nongovernmental organizations, or corporate leaders themselves. Although the business community frequently derides government regulators, pressure from these sources can help responsible corporate behavior migrate from the structural frontier to the civil foundation.

Consider, for instance, the case of mandatory air bags in automobiles. If only one manufacturer had decided to equip its vehicles with air bags, it would likely have had to raise sticker prices by $500 to $800. Without similar price increases by its rivals, the manufacturer would have lost sales without creating an off-setting societal benefit. But by mandating air bags on all passenger cars, US regulators reduced traffic fatalities while they eliminated the transfer of purchases from one manufacturer to another.

Too bad so few regulations produce such happy outcomes. Some US pollution-control guidelines, for instance, have been estimated to cost society $1 billion per life saved. Were such inefficiencies to occur on the strategic frontier, they would be quickly disciplined by the marketplace. But erroneous judgments in the structural frontier often face less scrutiny and can therefore remain in force indefinitely, creating a societal cost that ultimately diminishes the civil foundation. For that reason, before they impose a requirement on business, regulators should be sure to establish metrics that enable them to assess whether a regulation's value exceeds its cost. Failure to do so can have the wholly unintended effect of shrinking the civil foundation by causing a dramatic slowdown in economic progress.

That's precisely what has happened in British Columbia over the past two decades. In their attempt to compel corporations toward socially responsible behavior, regulators have imposed so many costs and administrative burdens on businesses that many simply decamped for friendlier climes. As a result, B.C. has suffered a marked slowing in the improvement of living standards, working conditions, and real income—hardly the outcome sought by regulators.

NGOs that wish to exert effective pressure on corporations can learn an important lesson from this example: they must be careful not to tip over into extremism or to advance agendas that lack popular support. Those cautions aside, the successes of NGOs can't be denied. It was primarily pressure from NGOs that convinced oil companies to withdraw their support of the corrupt and despotic Abacha regime in Nigeria, and that helped improve working conditions in Southeast Asia.

But perhaps the most effective pressure on corporate leaders will be the pressure they impose on themselves. To date, the US government has given no sign that it will force energy producers, utilities, and heavy industries to reduce their output of greenhouse gases. And no single corporation can be expected to do so alone, since the attendant costs would dwarf any marginal improvement in public health and safety. If any action is to be taken, it will have to come from a corporate coalition assembled by an intrinsically motivated leader with the energy, vision, and communication skills necessary to convince other corporate leaders to take a sizable risk.

Such leadership is also required to address globalization's most troublesome dilemma—that is, the inconsistency among the world's civil foundations. The lack of global standards can hobble attempts at collective action on the structural frontier. Consider the Foreign Corrupt Practices Act, for example. The act attempts to universalize a feature of the US civil foundation by prohibiting bribery overseas by a country's corporations. For the most part, the act has maintained a level playing field for US corporations as they go after foreign business. But many complain that the act puts them at a disadvantage compared with corporations from countries where bribes are considered just another cost of doing business.

Imagine the difficulty corporations and countries will encounter as they grapple with the question of global warming. Already, countries with relatively undeveloped civil foundations protest that they're being held to the environmental standards of advanced economies, which in turn complain that companies in countries with shallow civil foundations enjoy an unfair cost advantage over their more socially responsible rivals. And while this squabbling goes on, the threat posed by global warming only increases. Ultimately, the logjam will be broken only when courageous and intrinsically motivated corporate leaders promote the notion of a global civil foundation that businesses, together with governments and NGOs, work constantly to upgrade.

Applying the Virtue Matrix to Your Business

Before we start talking about next steps you can take starting today, let's review: The bottom half of the Virtue Matrix is the *civil founda-tion*, which represents the current cultural norms, laws, regulations, and customs of a given nation or industry. These have been built up over time as an economy advances. In some countries, this half of the matrix is quite robust, while in others it is more fragile or even lack-ing. Think of child-labor laws and how they came into existence in developed countries but may be altogether absent in other regions of the world. The civil foundation's *choice* quadrant isn't regulated by law but more by culture and expectation. Its *compliance* quadrant is what it sounds like: responsible actions that a corporation would be forced to do anyway or face legal penalties.

The top half of the Virtue Matrix, the *frontier* represents all the issues and activities that have yet to become part of the norms, laws, regulations, and customs of a society. They may present risks and or opportunities to companies who participate in them. Companies often move within the frontier ahead of others in their industry in an-ticipation of regulations yet to come, or to distinguish themselves from their peers, or because of an intrinsic value dearly held by their officers. The frontier's *strategic* quadrant houses actions that are in-tended to be profitable but are still deemed good for society. The *structural* quadrant is focused on the common good but not an in-crease in shareholder wealth. Structural-quadrant actions might even decrease a company's assets.

The Goal

The strategy is to get a company to a place where it is fully compliant, where it tracks and leads other companies in terms of choice, and where it has identified and taken on key strategic- and structural-frontier initiatives.

The Process

This is a fairly intensive planning regimen and should, where possible, be connected to the company's ongoing strategic, even divisional planning processes. It is necessary to create a team to generate the appropriate information and to comprehend the current situation or to make recommendations about the future. This team needs a leader who reports directly to the CEO or COO. The work group should be cross-disciplinary and from all divisions of the company, functional as well as regional.

The team will create a set of priorities and actions among relevant social issues that supports the firm and integrate the appropriate information by linking to business strategy. This is critical and will keep a team focused on new issues, ideas, and influences as they emerge. The third need is to assess the state of play in the industry across the four quadrants of the Virtue Matrix. Only then can a team identify and prioritize potential corporate citizenship initiatives looking ahead.

The Compliance Quadrant: All companies already have some compliance in place, but are you fully compliant? If a company is not fully in compliance it will literally be impossible to realize any returns on investments in other corporate citizenship initiatives. Getting compliance in shape is a first and relatively easy step. Think about The Gap and what it cost them to discover that their own supply chain was out of compliance. Or worse, recall Arthur Anderson and the charges brought against them after their auditing of Enron. The cost of being out of compliance is simply too high to bear.

The Choice Quadrant: Beyond laws and regulations, most companies generally participate in a number of voluntary citizenship activities related to both the community and philanthropy. Many also practice adherence to voluntary industry standards, product development, responsible sourcing, environmental footprint reduction, and corporate citizenship commitments and reporting. Ask yourself if your company adheres to or exceeds industry and cultural norms and conventions. Is it a leader or a follower with regard to community relations, encouraging volunteerism, and philanthropy? Do you meet all the industry standards in your given industry associations? Are you listed on the responsible company indices? Is the firm involved in voluntary initiatives such as the United Nations Global Compact, or does it comply with the Global Reporting Initiative? If the company operates internationally, does it apply a single philosophy, or apply different standards around the world? How does it work with local mores and conventions? Is there a consistent experience with the company, no matter where a branch is located?

A challenge of globalization that many companies have experienced is that it allows companies to choose to operate in environments without a strong civil foundation. This may lower costs, but it also often lowers compliance standards. Like Novartis, your company may find it advantageous to operate at high standards wherever the company does business. Think of the cost to textile and clothing manufacturing in countries like Bangladesh where standards have been sacrificed.

The Strategic Quadrant: This area of the frontier is the greatest for differentiation, and a hotbed of innovation. Great reputations are made here, and advancements can change entire industries. Often, successful initiatives within this quadrant are copied by others. Toyota's branding and product innovation is an example, and other companies have been trying to catch up. Your company needs to identify which issues and initiatives best fit your organization. They have to contribute to your key relationships and benefit your interests and communities. Think of Ericsson and its work on disaster response or Novo Nordisk on diabetes, as good examples.

The Structural Quadrant: In this domain, firms solve problems working jointly on solutions, as no one company could solve an issue without costing more than the value it creates. Toy makers, for instance, have demanded better testing. Other industries have asked for better regulation and enforcement. Think of Swiss cement maker Holcim and its industry-wide initiative on lowering CO_2 emissions.

Case studies with companies who have employed the Virtue Matrix suggest that scope is tricky; allies are all important; wise choosing of team members is critical; finding common ground is not always easy; research is time consuming and challenging; and analysis is required to develop real insights.

Based on all the information and analysis a company can now generate a long list of potentially valuable initiatives. Begin to sort the issues into the four quadrants of the Virtue Matrix. Ask, with which issues should the firm comply? With which should it choose to only meet industry standards? What few issues should the firm consider engaging in beyond compliance requirements and industry norms—both individually (on the strategic frontier) and with other companies (on the structural frontier)?

This sorting process encompasses many variables, involves many players, and can be global in design. Hence there are no right or single answers. This is a dynamic process with issues effecting other issues. The end result is a portfolio of various priorities that can guide a company on what is important and where to make investments. The result of this first part of the process is *insight*. You discover what has to be managed, your positioning options, and where the company can lead, follow, or cruise in the middle of the pack. The goal is to unearth where you could add significant and distinctive value and the best opportunities for collaborative action among industry players.

Deciding on Action

At this point you will need to get specific. What can/should you actually do? You will need to work out the details for each quadrant.

Compliance means confirmed, reportable data attesting that the company is in fact compliant. This is best gathered by outside third parties who can provide more and unbiased information to your stakeholders. This kind of consulting doesn't come cheap, but a prudent company goes beyond mere compliance and seeks out opportunities to add value by improving data, managing costs, and perfecting processes. If in doubt about compliance, double check, and get the best professional advice and counsel your firm can afford.

For each issue in the **Choice** quadrant, the team should recommend a desired position among competitors and a rationale for that positioning. An action plan should be brought forward, and a key executive should be held responsible and accountable for its implementation.

For each issue in the **Strategic** frontier, a team must dig deeper and develop a business plan to clarify how the issue relates to the company and to outline possible approaches and assess potential value: returns, risks, and costs. What is the most important issue that was brought up? Who could be helped? What tactics will we employ to achieve the desired outcome? What is distinctive about what we will do? Who will reward the company for the actions, and how? What is needed to achieve this? A budget should be drawn up. Use analysis to decide and select the leading initiatives. Demote the remainder to the choice quadrant.

For each issue in the **Structural** frontier, the team needs to outline where to place the project and who will have accountability. You will need to engage other companies or other interests such as government or NGOs and find the necessary resources. These are complicated issues, as they involve coordination of multiple parties with different interests and time horizons. The key is to focus on issues that are yet to be widely accepted but where joint action is necessary—or in which regulation may be inevitable.

Taking Action

This is not a checklist process, since there are so many moving parts and variables. Personalities, external pressures, and only so much time and resources come into play. Your corporate citizenship priorities have to fit into the company's overall priorities and governance processes. Every company is different. Know what fits and what doesn't. Don't simply bolt on new initiatives; rather, fit them into the way you do things. Expectations will be high, both internally and externally. It is never easy to take action, and there will be surprises. This is your chance to choose, to act, and hopefully to emerge as a paradigm of corporate citizenship.

Conclusion

Mapping out a company's future and guiding it there is a real challenge. The range of issues is becoming more and more complex. This is true for all companies and all industries. The Virtue Matrix gives a company conceptual tools and a step-by-step process to understand key issues and to act on them. Rather than responding defensively, as many corporations do, you will be able to confidently answer questions about what you are doing and why. There are challenges, and this is an evolving field, but a company using these tools should be more hopeful about the potential impact it can have looking ahead. I'm convinced that most business leaders sincerely wish to meet the high expectations of the noblest in society, if not exceed it, and the Virtue Matrix is designed to aid them in their efforts. While it cannot resolve or eliminate the competing claims of shareholders, society, and the government, the matrix offers a framework for evaluating those claims and encourages business leaders to be as bold and innovative in enriching society as they are in enriching their shareholders.

NOTES

1. This chapter owes much to the work of Roger Martin—former dean of the University of Toronto's Rotman School of Business and trusted strategy

advisor to CEOs of major corporations around the world—who created the Virtue Matrix. Our application of it here is used with his permission. For the original article introducing the Virtue Matrix, see Roger L. Martin, "The Virtue Matrix: Calculating the Return on Corporate Responsibility," *Harvard Business Review* 80, no. 3 (March 2002): 68–75. Or request reprint R0203E.

2. Michael E. Porter and Mark Kramer, "The Competitive Advantage of Corporate Philanthropy," *Harvard Business Review* 80, no. 12 (December 2002): 56–68.

CHAPTER 7

A DISAPPOINTMENT, A TURNAROUND, A SMART STEP, AND A FRESH START

The Solent is a strait that separates the Isle of Wight off southern England from the mainline coast with its busy port of Southampton. It is about fifteen miles long and four miles across at its widest point. It is the major channel for lots of very large commercial and military vessels. Given its tidal geography, shallow depths, and strong winds, it can be very precarious, if not dangerous—even if you know what you are doing. The Titanic departed through the Solent, and so have many other famous ships down the centuries that did not make it to their final destinations.

Looking out over the Solent from high land, you see hundreds of large ships navigating the narrow strait. You notice the rocks above water and the pebble beach to one side—as well as many shifting sandbars—but not what lurks below the surface. You know that steering the rudder on such large and valuable vessels requires a combination of true skill and patience, of fortitude and foresight. It is hard to turn a large ship, particularly in a strait, and the effects take time and real planning. That is why such waters often deploy pilots to assist inexperienced captains. Making a mistake can be costly—in economic and in human terms.

Driving a big company or a government institution is not much different. The channels of navigation are fairly well known, and making changes and managing them to success is very hard work. It takes time to adjust course, and often, the lapses are overcome by the next fad or yet another crisis. If you get too far off track, you're in trouble. Steering a so-called turnaround, as the word is used in business circles, is nearly impossible, which is why so few occur. Companies merge, divest, and start new units more easily than totally turning around an existing business. Strategies may come and go, and tactics often shift by the quarterly calendar, but taking an established company (or government office) in an entirely new and different direction is rare, very rare, indeed.

In this and the next chapter, we present to you five examples, in light of the truths of common sense. One started out navigating in the right direction but veered off course. Another achieved a successful turnaround. A third is a smart move by a government toward a brighter horizon. And fourth shines as a newer ship in the sea that is on the right track. Finally in chapter 8, there's the global business that started out with common sense and is still on course—proving that even a huge freighter can remain steered straight when it follows the right guiding stars.

The Disappointment: Prudential

The Rock of Gibraltar is the symbol of Prudential Financial, Inc. It was chosen to reflect the strength and security that the company offers its customers. "Get a Piece of the Rock," is the familiar tagline from decades past, so often seen in dramatic television commercials or in colorful print advertisements all across the United States.

Prudential Financial was originally given a very comforting name, which sounded more like a charity than the burial insurance company it was: The Widows and Orphans Friendly Society. For just three cents a week, burial and funeral insurance could be purchased by working-class people, whose finances would be devastatingly affected by a husband/father's death. Founded in Newark, New Jersey, in 1875 by John Fairfield Dryden (who later became a US senator), it became the Prudential Friendly Society, then Prudential Insurance. As a mutual company owned by its customers, it expanded to sell other forms of affordable policies.

Today, "The Pru"—as it is colloquially called—is more than 135 years old, and it has grown considerably in its business of wealth protection. With 47,000 employees, over $1.3 trillion in assets, and $3.5 trillion in gross life insurance in force in forty-one countries, this company is a behemoth in the financial services industry. Prudential's primary services and products today are life insurance, annuities, retirement-related products and services, mutual funds, and investment management. It still operates mostly in the United States, but no longer to those living paycheck to paycheck. Its main markets are mass middle, mass affluent, and affluent. And it's no longer a mutual company but rather publically traded (as PRU of course) and answerable to stockholders.

When you read the company prospectus and eyeball its websites, you are told it strives for long-term value through strong fundamentals guided by its core values: "We are committed to keeping our promises and doing business the right way." Indeed, Prudential remains one of the most trusted brands, even if "the Rock" has taken a few dents and chips over the years. Surveys show it is still considered a relative icon of strength, stability, and expertise. But its reputation has noticeably slipped.

Prudential advertises well their commitment to ethical actions. For them this involves a code of conduct with ethical filters for decision making, raising questions, reporting concerns, acting ethically, complying with the law, managing risk, and treating people fairly. The core values at Prudential have been refined over the years and now revolve around being a trusted brand that is differentiated by top talent and innovative solutions. Just four core values bind the global company together: worthy of trust, customer focus, respect for others, and winning. Yes, winning! Winning—a competitive rather than cooperative maxim—has now crept in as a core value.

In terms of good governance, The Pru positions itself as uncompromising in integrity and committed to shareholder and stakeholder engagement as well as sustainability and environmental stewardship.

Since 2012, the company has issued an annual sustainability report; a recent one was entitled "Keeping Our Promises."

On corporate responsibility, Prudential stresses that they are committed to the communities where they "live and work." Like other such companies, Prudential has a corporate foundation that awards grants funded by the company. It has also more recently become a social investor in a variety of forms for both profit and not-for-profit organizations. In their language, they are "creating social impact while earning an appropriate risk-adjusted return."

With an emphasis on volunteering, the company has an employee-engagement program that deploys the expertise of its employees into communities in need. The largest such outreach is in the impoverished city of Newark, where the company is still headquartered.

On paper and in its own print, Prudential sounds like a laudable—even exemplar—company, deeply rooted in ethics and doing good, common-sense business. From its name, you would have to surmise that it always was and forever will aspire to be a prudent company.

Cracks in the Rock

Yet something has gone terribly wrong. The more recent history of the company called Prudential no longer seems all that prudent. To quote Pogo in the cartoons, "We have met the enemy, and he is us." Unfortunately, the simple, straight answer is that Prudential divorced itself from practicing common-sense prudence as an insurer. From their founding, they had persevered and prospered for a very long time, through all kinds of business cycles. And they had stellar business performance for much of that life. Why is that? It is because for many, many years, Prudential was wonderfully boring—prudent, patient, principled, and practical. They were safe, tried and true.

Then at some point, the company totally changed direction. Prudential wanted to compete with the big banks and investment firms. Greed and avarice took over. They shifted their old business model from risk-aversion and long-term growth to a new model of risk-aggressive and short-term profit maximization.

After converting from a mutual company to a stock company in order to pursue these new ambitious goals, the management became preoccupied with its stock price and quarterly earnings. Short-term gratification replaced long-term stability. And in the process, Prudential lost contact with decades of customer focus, most of their founding principles, and—in consequence—much credibility and customer loyalty.

Eventually, even their profitability took a hit. Breaking bonds of trust with their consumer base had negative consequences on nearly every front. Bad and costly acquisitions, like the securities firm Bache and a large realty group, failed to deliver the desired results. Far worse, they brought sizeable losses, complexity, and lawsuits.

The lesson of this tale is that the virtue of prudence so ensconced in the very name of the company can be lost overnight. The boring or perhaps just old-fashioned concept of common-sense business behavior, where one abides by the four Ps, was gambled away and never fully recouped. Today, Prudential is prudent in name only. Whereas prudence implies conservatism, consistency, stability, and reliability, more recent years of Prudential's dealings have been all but that. These unfortunately are no longer part of Prudential (or for that matter, of most of the insurance industry). But of course, Prudential hasn't changed their hype or rewritten their history. They still tout their brand as before. Yet, most have caught on to what they're truly after and consider them peddlers of face advertising. Thus the company disappoints twice. First because of its unstable ways of doing business, and second because it breaks the very principles it proclaims. And hypocrisy does not attract customers, nor is it founded in common sense. Perhaps the company would be better renamed Imprudential?

The Turnaround: Interface

After reading *The Ecology of Commerce* by Paul Hawken, industrial radicalist (as he termed himself) Ray Anderson, the late CEO of Interface, Inc., reoriented his company from profit-maximization and market domination toward an environmentally sustainable, responsible enterprise. For the company's Mission Zero program and other initiatives, Anderson received multiple awards and distinctions. But the real story is that he actually turned his company around, and he did it without sacrificing profitability. Interface is now the world's largest carpet designer and maker of carpet tile.

Origins

Interface was born in 1973 when Anderson, a 1956 Georgia Tech graduate, recognized the need for floorcoverings that were more flexible for modern offices. He led a joint venture between Carpets International PLC in the UK and a group of American investors. Interface would produce and market what were essentially modular floorcoverings with soft surfaces.

On its first day of operation, the new company had just a handful of employees, including Anderson, and faced significant challenges from sharply rising petrochemical costs (a key raw material in the carpet industry). But advancements in cutting and bonding technology kept the company going through the office-building boom of the1970s. Modular carpet tiles grew in popularity, and the company went public in 1983.

Through acquisitions, Interface gained entry into the European and Middle Eastern markets. They expanded their product line and services. Over the years, the company's growth has been augmented by more than fifty acquisitions. It entered the residential market in 2003 with the introduction of FLOR, a custom modular-rug company. It has sales in 110 countries and manufacturing facilities on four continents. *Fortune* called Interface one of "America's Most Admired Companies" and one of the "100 Best Companies to Work For."

The Epiphany

Reading *The Ecology of Commerce* completely changed Anderson's outlook on business. He had been widely successful already, but he discovered that something important was missing from his business. He found particularly convincing the concept of merging good business practices with common-sense environmental concerns. In 1994, with Interface already a twenty-one-year-old company, Anderson formally challenged the entire company to pursue a bold new vision: "Be the first company that, by its deeds, shows the entire world what sustainability is in all its dimensions: people, process, product, place, and profits—and in doing so, become restorative through the power of influence." Ray fought constantly to reach his audacious goals. As the turnaround progressed, a passion for sustainability took hold with the company's people—and it was transformed from the inside out. Interface became one of Forbes "100 Best Corporate Citizens," and in 2006, GlobeScan listed it as number one in the world for corporate sustainability.

The changes that Anderson initiated did impact the company's financial performance in the short term. The initial costs were high, in fact, but they paid off by creating a lasting, sustainable enterprise.

A Profound Course Correction

New ways of thinking offered a fresh perspective on product design. Interface worked with the Biomimicry Institute, which uses nature as a model for developing sustainable solutions, to apply biomimicry thinking in product development. For instance, by asking how nature designs a floor, Interface developed the i2 line of products—including Entropy, one of the most specified products—inspired by the "organized chaos" of the forest floor. (The design allows small portions of carpet to be replaced one at a time without changing the look of the design. It allows carpet from areas of higher use to be switched out with less-worn parts. Everyone benefits, from the customer to the planet.) In addition, inspired by the many examples in nature of adhesion without glue, Interface developed Tactile, a carpet-tile installation system that uses small adhesive squares to connect carpet without the need for glue.

Life Cycle Assessment (LCA) is another tool used by the company to evaluate the environmental aspects associated with a product or process. It captures the materials, energy, and wastes involved in each phase, from raw-materials extraction to recycling or final disposal. Besides toxicity and resource depletion, LCA can even measure global-warming potential. By comparing LCA results of different products or processes, Interface can choose the one that has the lower environmental impact.

Interface also developed strategies for dematerialization and the use of recycled materials to reach its goals. Dematerialization at Interface is the process of making the same-quality product using less material. It can be achieved by using existing materials more efficiently or by substituting with alternative ones.

Interface's shift in values manifested itself in the company's social activities, programs, and actions—in all the ways it conducted business, and with all its stakeholders. Interface fosters a fair, friendly, and inclusive corporate culture where every associate has a responsibility to do his or her part to help reduce its environmental footprint. The company also encourages employee volunteering in the communities in which it does business, and they donate to local organizations that share their values.

"Mission Zero" is Interface's endeavor to have zero negative impact on the natural environment. It's "Renewable by 2020" goal is part of Mission Zero. It would mean that all energy used by the company would be, by the year 2020, gained from renewable resources. Interface has implemented several unique energy-saving measures in its factories. For example, the energy-monitoring system used in its Scherpenzeel factory in the Netherlands is called the Energy Mirror. It tracks real-time energy use and prominently displays the results, allowing employees at all levels to identify ways to reduce use. The company has also replaced and upgraded equipment, including HVAC units and lighting systems, with more efficient alternatives and installed skylights and solar tubes to reduce the need for electric lighting during the daytime. All of the efficiencies, improvements, and most importantly, kilowatts not used add up to significant progress since this all began in 1994. Total energy use at Interface's global factories is down 39 percent per unit of product since 1996. As of 2013, five of their seven factories were operating with 100 percent renewable electricity and 35 percent of total energy from renewable sources.

> *Still, they never lose sight of the bottom line. They stay ahead of the competition by constantly seeking new and more efficient processes. They increase shareholder value, but sustainably and in a reliable manner. And they lead by example, encouraging other firms to follow their lead.*
> —One Uncommon CEO with Common Sense

Ray Anderson effected Interface's redemptive U-turn and was critical to its turnaround. Can he be qualified as a common-sense business person? Most definitely. He demonstrated the four Ps of common-sense business, and when you read his biography, collected thoughts, and the documentaries about him, you see a character-based style of servant leadership that is prudent, wise, and responsible. But it is also bold and innovative; it breaks the existing mold. If we were to place his actions during the turnaround into the Virtue Matrix (see chapter 6), we'd see that he considered the "civil foundation" to be only the minimum effort. He pushed out into the "frontier" in both *strategic* and *structural* ways. For instance, "Interface supports fundamental human rights for all people, and is committed to complying with employment laws in every country in which it operates." That's from

Interface's official core-values documents. However, the statement doesn't end there. Anderson didn't stay in the civil foundation but led his company out into the frontier: "Interface strives to create an organization wherein all people are accorded unconditional respect and dignity; one that allows each person to continuously learn and develop."

Again, their core values don't stop in the civil foundation when it comes to discrimination. Yes, "Interface supports and upholds the elimination of discriminatory practices with respect to employment and occupation and respects diversity within its business operations." But it goes beyond what's regulated to make an impact through its example and practices by emphasizing that the company "further supports the elimination of all forms of forced, bonded, or compulsory labor" and "supports the elimination of exploitative child labor."

Interface is a successful model of a responsible turnaround to sustainability. But it didn't reach this success by staying safely behind the walls of the civil foundation. Its journey documents a path forward for common-sense business leaders and companies with the courage to follow. If you are interested in turning your own ship around, see the tools in part III of this book to help you get started.

The Smart Move: New UK Authorities

Any organization, society, or nation needs guidance and some degree of regulation. Banks require such regulatory framework in order to maintain fairness in an economy and to protect against risk, at both the level of the system and of the individual institution. In the United Kingdom, there are two important authoritative programs that have been brought forward, post-financial-crisis, to provide such fairness and protection. We want to highlight them here as epitomes of common sense, because the UK is essentially palisading their own camp for the next time the financial-crisis wolves show up. The two programs are called the FCA (Financial Conduct Authority) and the PRA (Prudential Regulation Authority), and they work together to protect both customers and firms.

The FCA is a legislated program set up by the government according to the Financial Services Act of 2012. This act of Parliament created a new "regulatory framework for the financial system and financial services in the UK," according to government documents. When the FCA, created on April 1, 2013, replaced what had been called the Financial *Services* Authority, a new emphasis was prioritized: to ensure that consumers are treated fairly. Fair treatment of consumers means that they are not mistreated or misinformed, they are protected from dishonesty and fraud, and they have a way to complain if necessary.

Not only is it imperative that consumers be treated fairly, but firms of any size must conduct themselves appropriately for the economy to function properly as a whole. So the FCA also serves as a protective initiative for financial markets through its enhancement of the entire financial system. Given the near market collapse and the bank bailouts, the FCA works to encourage "effective competition" in the hopes of maintaining confidence in the UK economy. Overall, the FCA regulates some 56,000 financial-services firms. It is designed as an "independent public body" and receives funding through service fees from the firms that it guides and polices.

The FCA prides itself on "putting...protection above profits." One way this is done is through monitoring the firms and people who enter the market and by requiring them to reach certain standards before the authorization to sell or trade is granted. If a firm or individual does not meet the given standards, then the FCA acts to shut down their activities. Overall, the purpose is to make sure that all consumers feel financially and otherwise safe and that there is sufficient market competition. A trusting bond between the customer and the firm is vital in making the economy work, and the FCA sets the parameters for that trust.

Just like the FCA, the PRA was designed through the Financial Services Act of 2012. But unlike the independent FCA, the PRA is a part of the Bank of England.

The Bank of England is the central bank of the country and is also known as the "Old Lady of Threadneedle Street," where it is located. The main goal of the Bank is to encourage the "good of the people" by keeping a sound and stable financial system. The well-established Bank of England and the newcomer PRA work together—alongside the Bank's Financial Policy Committee and Special Resolution Unit—to "promote the safety and soundness of financial firms." The PRA's second objective is aimed at insurers, and its role is "to contribute to securing an appropriate degree of protection for policyholders." With these goals in mind, the PRA takes three approaches: judgment-based, forward-looking, and focused. The judgment approach has a single purpose, namely, to determine whether firms are safe and stable and to set the level of protection needed to meet certain conditions. The forward-looking approach is to make sure that there are no risks that the firm is facing and to solve the issues assessed as highest risk, based on prudent action. The focused approach looks at issues and firms that have the largest risk when it comes to overall UK financial stability. As a whole, the PRA is "responsible for the prudential regulation and supervision of about 1,700 banks, building societies, credit unions, insurers, and major investment firms."

The PRA supervises a great number of "deposit takers," whose contribution to and effects on the economy are extensive. There are two sectors of supervision: banking and insurance. Within the two sectors, the PRA has different expectations and rules, which are expected to be met and followed to the letter of the law. Firms must conduct business with integrity, skill, care, and diligence. They must act in a prudent manner and maintain financial resources, as well as staying organized and effective. Lastly, firms must be ready for important issues that might arise, and have a resolution at hand. As for management and governance, each firm's board is expected to manage the firm properly and to make sure that it is safe, sound, and stable through "prudent management and governance." When it comes to PRA's enforcement of its regulations, it mainly works to prevent and mitigate long-term, noncyclical or systemic risks. However, the PRA does also have power to impose financial penalties on a firm that it judges irresponsible or delinquent.

Although they serve two different purposes and receive funding differently, both of these new UK authorities spring from the same effort and actually work well together. The FCA and the Bank (PRA), for instance, both value efficient regulatory reporting processes. So in order to avoid duplicated information, the two authorities share data, and firms therefore only report to them once—a reality appreciated at every level, we're sure.

We loudly applaud the UK's use of common-sense efforts, through these two authorities, to avoid another financial slump, crash, or full-on disaster. Surely the entire globe will benefit from their actions.

The Fresh Start: Prudent Energy

It is not only because of its name, "Prudent Energy," that this company naturally deserves to feature in this book. It is because the firm lives up to its name. What is it about this unique, young energy company that makes it, well, so commonsensical?

Energy fuels our global economy. It is the lifeblood that makes everything happen. Without energy, the economy would come to a halt. Energy consumption, especially of a polluting type, is, of course, part of our problem. More sustainable solutions are therefore sought on every front. But to what extent should a company "go green"? What would that imply, for instance, for a utility company or a national grid?

In order to answer such questions, further issues need to be considered: Are renewables ever really going to take off and switch us out of our dependence on petroleum? What is the role of politics in these markets? Some countries like Japan, Germany, Switzerland, and Sweden have decided against a nuclear future. Others subsidize or give tax credits to renewables. Wind and solar power are gradually gaining greater acceptance. Some states, like California, have stricter environmental standards than the countries they are part of—will they or their mother countries set the standard for the future?

This much seems clear: Wind and solar power are gradually gaining greater acceptance. And many analysts hold that one key to a more sustainable energy future lies in perfecting batteries that can collect and store energy within reach. Lithium batteries are increasingly being used in smaller devices and in cars to power engines and store power, but you would need a much larger battery for industrial uses.

That's where Prudent Energy fits in. Its theme is "Unleash the power of energy storage." Prudent Energy designs, manufacturers, and integrates the patented Vanadium Redox Battery (VRB). This long-life storage system is also environmentally friendly.

How does the VRB work? It balances energy flow by warehousing electricity loads, bridging from one generation plant to another, while continuously maintaining voltage and frequency. This is particularly useful for cases requiring megawatt hours of energy for long duration, ramping, peak shaving and peak shifting. Put simply, Prudent Energy reduces energy use. But how can reducing the need for your product actually increase your profits? Isn't that working yourself out of a job? Not if you are placing yourself strategically on the Virtue Matrix (see chapter 7). Prudent Energy sells or leases its products to industrial and commercial users and various generators of all sizes to reduce operating expenses and lower utility bills. So they are attractive to energy consumers. And since energy *storage* is the major focus in the energy business these days, Prudent Energy has put themselves both on the cutting edge and in the sweet spot.

As a privately owned company in the early stages of development, Prudent Energy benefits from having some very prominent investors, including the likes of CEL Partners, Draper Fisher Jurvetson, DT Capital, GS Energy, idVest, Jafco Ventures, Mitsui, Northern Light

VC, Sequoia Capital, and State Power Group, Ltd. This is a Who's Who list of backers who have a proven track record; these firms do not invest their money lightly. In other words, they have done their due diligence and believe in both the business plan and the management team at Prudent Energy.

Founded in 2007 and headquartered in Bethesda, Maryland, and Beijing, China, Prudent Energy has research and development facilities in the United States, Canada, and Asia. To its competitive advantage, it has international patents, registered trademarks, and some sixty US patents, including use with wind farms and off-grid and smart-grid applications. The company acquired the assets of VRB Power Systems in 2009, which is the key technology.

What Prudent Energy has is seen as a *sustainable solution* to power generation. This is a frontrunner technology with great potential in the renewable energy sector. It is spreading its wings while perfecting its designs and products.

Now you may be asking, aside from the hype, how is energy storage of this scaled type actually deployed? Some examples are in order. Consider Gills Onions, a food-processing firm based in Oxnard, California. It uses tons of energy for refrigeration and processing of over a million pounds of onions a day. By investing in a gigantic Prudent Energy battery the size of a tennis court, it is saving on energy costs and treating the environment more humanely. Prudent Energy provided the long-term solution to its needs that saves money *and* ups their "common good" factor.

The China Electric Power Company in Zhangbei, Hebei province, used Prudent Energy to solve their particular problem. Their wind-power integration project into the state grid of China needed a high level of technical know-how and the right product fit. Prudent Energy came through with the installation of a 1 megawatt hour energy-storage system rated at a peak of 750 kilowatts pulse capability.

What these and other examples show is that Prudent Energy can help integrate renewable energy into power networks to ensure grid stability. It has vast industrial and commercial application around the globe. The future of the grid lies in such innovative and prudent systems.

With its systems now installed in the United States, China, Kenya, Hungary, Turkey, and Italy, Prudent Energy is showing the way to a different kind of energy future. Named as a Global Cleantech company in 2010, the accolades keep coming. What might not be as obvious at first glance is that this company is benefiting from a common-sense approach to business, including a patient, long-term perspective and prudent use of resources. It isn't ironic at all that an energy company named "Prudent" is in fact making our energy use so much more prudent. They truly embody this first P of common-sense business.

CHAPTER 8

CARGILL: BUILDING TRUST

Common sense is genius dressed in its working clothes.
—Ralph Waldo Emerson

Cargill is an international producer and marketer of agricultural, financial, and industrial products and services. It was founded in 1865 when W.W. Cargill, a former captain in the supply corps of the Union Army, took the railroad to the end of the line at Conover, Iowa. While his intention was to farm there, Mr. Cargill found the price of land too high and opted instead to build a grain-storage and shipping facility. The company now employs over 160,000 people in sixty-eight countries. In 2015, Cargill had $130.4 billion in sales and other revenues. Net earnings were $1.56 billion. Not surprisingly, Cargill has been for years either the largest or second-largest privately held company in the world.

Midwestern and Presbyterian

W.W. Cargill was a Midwesterner, and he was a Christian—specifically, a Presbyterian. His company has taken on the character of its founder. In typical Midwestern fashion, W.W. wasn't interested in the fastest or the flashiest. He exercised prudence in his business, and his common-sense, practical wisdom has built the vast powerhouse that his family carries on today.

Midwestern values include being friendly, honest, and authentic—and most importantly, having integrity. Presbyterian values might be said to include education, life-long learning, and hard work.

Presbyterians prioritize the putting of one's faith into practice; your beliefs have to influence how you operate in real life. Presbyterians emphasize generosity, hospitality, and the constant pursuit of justice and reform. These "spiritual traditions" shaped Cargill at its founding, and they follow it into the twenty-first century as part of its legacy.

Now, this isn't to say that Cargill is a religious company; it's not. It's not what you would call "faith-based," and they don't evangelize. But that doesn't mean that the prudent business practices inherent in the Presbyterian way of thinking don't permeate the things they do. In fact, these "spiritual traditions" are considered treasured assets of the company. The values that came out of the traditions were baked into the common-sense corporate culture that has been nurtured at Cargill.

The motto "Our word is our bond" began the company, and it persists today. We've included here a copy of an internal memo from November 5, 1975, in which Cargill refuses to "profit from any practice which is immortal or unethical." Not only would this go against the culture of the company, it would damage that which it considers priceless: its "fine reputation built on integrity."

CARGILL
Cargill Building
Minneapolis, Minnesota 55402   November 5, 1975
Whitney Macmillan
President

Fellow Employees:

During the past year, all of us have been made aware
through the news media of various illegal or questionable
corporate practices, ranging from illegal campaign
contributions in the U.S. to payoffs made to foreign
officials. Grain industry firms have been charged with
bribing weighers and inspectors at U.S. export elevators.
Such events compel me to reaffirm certain corporate
policies of Cargill as they apply to all of our
activities around the world.

Our corporate goals and objectives state: "Continue to
make certain that all employees of the Cargill Companies
recognize and adhere to the principles of integrity which
have always been basic to our philosophy and upon which
the Cargill Companies' reputation is founded."

1) This means we have a deep responsibility to conduct
    ourselves and our business under the highest standards
    of ethics, integrity, and in compliance with the laws
    of all countries and communities in which we have been
    granted the opportunity to perform our services.

2) This means should there be a question concerning a
    particular practice, open discussion will surely
    resolve the issue. If a practice cannot be discussed
    openly, it must be wrong.

3) This means business secured by any means other than
    legal, open, honest competition is wrong.

4) This means if a transaction cannot be properly
    recorded in the company books, subject to an
    independent audit, it must be wrong.

5) This means that Cargill does not want any profit from
    any practice which is immoral or unethical. Should we
    discover our business being done in any other than
    absolutely proper manner, disciplinary action will be
    taken.

A company with a good reputation is a good place to work.
Cargill has enjoyed 110 years of a fine reputation built
on integrity. We must maintain our honor and self-respect
as a basis for our continued growth and pride in the
Cargill Companies.

Sincerely,

Whitney Macmillan

The Success of Common Sense

Cargill operates in five related business segments that are *vertically integrated*. This means that they work together to supply what is needed to each other. The segments, then, "help" all the others, so that each one depends less on outside companies (and the unknowns that come from that) than if they were entirely independent. When it comes to supply and support, Cargill "keeps it in the family," as it were:

Agriculture services: Cargill provides crop and livestock producers worldwide with customized farm services and products. This is their first and primary enterprise.

Food ingredients: They serve food and beverage manufacturers, foodservice companies, and retailers with food and beverage ingredients and new food applications. This segment works closely with and is sourced by their agriculture services segment.

Origination and processing: They connect producers and users of grain, oilseeds, and other agricultural commodities through origination, processing, marketing, and distribution capabilities and services. Cargill's other segments also benefit from the efforts of this segment.

Risk management and financial: Cargill has branched out to provide customers (and of course their own segments) with risk-management and financial solutions in a number of world markets.

Industrial: Finally, Cargill supplies customers worldwide with salt and steel products and services, and they are always developing new industrial applications for agricultural feedstocks. This segment, also, has clear avenues for integration with the others.

In addition to their dexterous use of vertical integration, Cargill has mastered three core competencies that make it stand out as a model of sustainable business:

Supply-chain management: After 150 years of practice and of building connections, Cargill has few equals in the world when it comes to moving massive amount of materials (whether it's perishable food or hardened steel) from continent to continent or from farm to factory. They are continually thinking of ways to make their supply chains as efficient as possible. Sometimes this means improving their own processes; sometimes it means collaborating with other trusted companies. Because they have established a reputation for reliability, other companies look forward to working with them, and this increases their influence and potential in the industry.

Risk management: Cargill's supply chains would be too vulnerable to be sustainable if the company didn't stay on top of potential risks. So they always are thinking about what could go wrong. Is the risk in this or that area worth the potential gain? What can be done to decrease the chances of failure or of a disastrous "surprise"? They also watch out for risks of overspending. They keep costs within budget, putting aside money to be available for potential unplanned opportunities they might want to take advantage of.

Research and development: Cargill is always looking into new ways to enhance an existing product, improve their processes, reduce costs, or get an innovation to market faster than their competitors. They also offer these services to the clients who hire them as consultants.

But we're not talking about a boardroom full of people throwing out ideas and voting on them. Cargill employs a team of more than 1,300 people to research, develop, and think scientifically about challenges, in more than two hundred locations around the world.

Think about what these strengths mean for this company. As a massive corporation, Cargill has more "problems" spring up in one day than most small businesses face in a year. Let's say that they need to obtain a patent on a certain way to use a product. *And* they want to figure out the best way to use biofuels in their trucks that are transporting goods cross-country. *And* they need to learn if their Muslim customers in the Middle East feel the same way about a certain product or process as do their Catholic customers in South America.

The difference between an overly specialized company and Cargill is that Cargill doesn't have to hire a firm to help them find out these answers or solve these problems. They can do it themselves—and quickly—because over time, they have already invested in the people they need. Their law experts can handle the patent; their ecologists can handle the biofuel question; their social scientists in local areas can compare notes on customer opinions by region and culture.

In addition, when one area makes a discovery, the knowledge they gain is shared across all the areas. So if Cargill researchers in Africa learn something new about nutrition, the information is easily shared with Cargill farmers in the United States. Can you imagine the money and time that this saves? That savings means more resources available to make the business even better. Long-term, prudent planning on the part of Cargill has created a sustainable business that now has the influence and know-how to make major positive differences in the world.

Using Success for the Common Good

A newer motto of Cargill has become "Helping the world thrive," and they take this task as seriously as they do their profit margin.[1] Take, for instance, their cocoa crops in Africa. When demand for cocoa got to be more than the farmers (and the soil) could handle, they created Promise 2012, a pledge aimed to improve livelihoods of farmers, their families, and their communities while *also* securing a long-term, responsible supply of cocoa that wouldn't overtax the land. To date, 2,550 farmer field schools have been established to train 115,000 small-time farmers in Africa in how to sustainably improve crop quality while increasing their own income. Cargill's common-sense investment has now strengthened their infrastructure, made life better for their global neighbors, and guaranteed many more years of a product that customers will never stop demanding (this *is* chocolate we're talking about!).

How tragic would it have been if a company, abandoning all common sense, had simply pressured their farmers to make more, faster, cheaper? Customers would soon tire of the low-quality product, the farmers themselves would burn out, and the reputation of yet another US firm would have been soiled around the world.

Of course, to do the best business, as we all know, you have to have the best people *in* your business. But getting them there is only half the job; then you have to keep them. You could say that just like Cargill's business segments are vertically integrated, so are their career positions. Employees are trained to be leaders and are encouraged to progress in the company. And as these home-grown leaders rise in the ranks, guess what? The Cargill values rise up with them. When is the last time that you heard about on-the-job leadership training that emphasized the importance of living up to your mistakes? Here's how Cargill puts it in their recruitment documents:

> *Integrity:* It's important for leaders to be honest, trustworthy, and if they make a mistake, which we all do, they're the first to admit it.
>
> *Conviction:* With leadership also comes a strong vision that inspires others to rally around them and take action.
>
> *Courage:* Our leaders are risk-takers. They face adversity with courage, challenge the status quo, and champion new viewpoints.

Common Sense: The Cargill Way

There's a phrase that's passed around freely in this giant company: "The Cargill Way." It suggests integrity, honesty, and the other values that emanate from Cargill philosophies, but it's also about *common sense*. The conservative approach started by Cargill in its very earliest years shapes how they do business, and it's made up of two insights. The first is "know the risks." The second is "hedge your bets." As far as the four Ps of common sense discussed in part I of this book, "The Cargill Way" has *prudence* written all over it.

In fact, Cargill has become renowned for its so-called devil's advocacy style of management. This is not just a form of contrarian thinking (arguing for the sake of argument), but it's a way of *asking probing questions* to get to the bottom of things. It is cautionary but rigorous and leads the company to move or make a change only when they have good, sound, evidence-based answers. This management style was articulated in a detailed question-asking methodology and typology created at Cargill.

To keep itself practical and always responsive to needs, Cargill has long instigated a suggestion plan (called i2i) that has brought about hundreds of new solutions. When an employee has a suggestion or problem and submits it to leaders above them in Cargill, they avoid a lot of bureaucratic red tape, because these leaders already meet regularly to discuss these exact types of things. So if you are an employee at Cargill, you aren't "bothering" the bosses with your input. The bosses are already meeting to discuss issues, and they can add your issue to the list. This regular gathering of top officers in Cargill for the purposes of pondering options is yet another common-sense solution that seems so simple it's obvious. But how many companies employ it? How many have come up with any meaningful way to address issues brought up by others on the inside? Cargill uses their question-asking technique to this day, and they've never published a guide to it outside the firm. We can share with you, however, these outline points below:

Types of Questions and Their Descriptions
1. Factual question: a "W" question (who? what? when? where? why?)
2. Explanatory question: gathering more information
3. Justifying question: going deeper
4. Leading question: planting ideas
5. Hypothetical question: supposing something

6. Alternative question: presenting choices

7. Coordinating question: expressing agreement

Directions of Questions

1. Overhead questions are asked of a group.

2. Direct questions are asked of a specific person.

3. Relay questions refer to a person or group.

4. Reverse questions refer back to the questioner.

Questioning Techniques and Purposes

1. Clarifying: to gain meaning and understanding

2. Restating: to achieve two-way communication and agreement

3. Neutral: to encourage unbiased thinking

4. Reflecting: to analyze and handle emotions

5. Summarizing: to dispose of a problem

So how does Cargill demonstrate the four Ps of common sense described in chapter 1? We've already talked about their *prudence*. How about their *principles*? We've established that they have those in spades. Their *patient* approach to both capital and to trade led them to weather the storms of the great depression (when other businesses might have folded and taken their losses for the good of the owner alone). It also led them to supply the Soviet Union with grain in its years of dire need. Cargill's *practical* approaches to problem-solving, such as the regular meeting of leaders to discuss internal issues, has also led it to take well-calculated risks, such as when they opened their trade doors to China much earlier than did many of their competitors.

More Common Sense at Cargill

Cargill has their "Four Musts" that define how they govern themselves from the inside. Again, they seem simple enough...but that is because they are based on common sense! What could happen in your organization if these were your four musts?

1. Give customers what they want.
2. Always add value.
3. Listen to the employees.
4. Transfer know-how, especially globally across territories and cultures.

Cargill leadership takes this idea of listening to the employees very seriously. They call it "management from the bottom," and just like the rest of common-sense business thinking, it's rooted in both humility and prudence. But it's still bottom-line practical. Happy employees mean happy customers, which means profits; that's not rocket science. By taking the voices of its people as a starting point, Cargill avoids the pitfalls of focusing only on short-term financial profitability, which prevails at so many other large companies.

Over time, this listening orientation has led to a movement for greater employee stock ownership in the company. Today some 17 percent of common stock has been allocated to and taken up by Cargill employees. For Cargill it seemed only commonsensical to allow its employees to benefit from and with the firm.

In the 1990s, the great business guru C.K. Prahalad assisted the Cargill leadership in an approach called "strategic intent." He helped them to investigate all the ways that their disparate business units could be even more closely integrated. Were two different parts of Cargill wasting time doing the same job? Were there places where poor communication between parts was leading to confusion and lost time? Were some parts not being used to their full potential because it was just the way it had always been done? You can bet that this work from Prahalad was costly to obtain. But Cargill saw it as an investment. This too was an exercise in strategic common sense.

Finally, a strong emphasis at Cargill has always been on *simplification*. "Complexity reduction" has become a mantra at this large organization, which—now operating on every continent—would otherwise be in danger of getting too complicated for its own good. In this spirit, eleven pages of fine print have been turned into a clear, crisply worded document now known as Cargill's *Basic Beliefs*. A few of their listed values include the following:

- Informal vs. formal organization
- Management by walking around
- Teamwork
- Serving basic needs
- Ethics and integrity
- Staying private [as opposed to publicly held]
- Being global
- Forming a single culture
- A humanistic approach to customers and employees
- Growing the business
- Having fun

These common-sense Midwestern values have served as a compass to guide the company. And since the values of the upper tiers are integrated into the everyday work experience of each and every employee, they become intertwined as the very DNA of the giant firm. The Cargill Way, synonymous with prudence as a virtue, demonstrates that common sense for the common good can also be a competitive advantage. We can't argue with that kind of success.

NOTES

1. For myriad intriguing examples, visit www.cargill.com/150/en.

CHAPTER 9

A POINT ABOUT PEOPLE

*Intuition is always right in at least two important ways; It is always
in response to something. It always has your best interest at heart.*
—Gavin de Becker

Too often, leaders think of the employees who work in a company—
small or large, public or private—as *resources* and tend to then neglect
or even abuse them. Some companies feign appreciation for their people, calling human resources their "most important assets," as if the people were cattle or some sort of disposable properties. They hire, fire, and
move around these "human assets" like so many pieces in a puzzle, rather
than as individuals with human personalities.

The best companies, like those we have illustrated in this book,
don't treat or think of their employees in this way. Based on common
sense and a richer sense of human dignity, they instead have the utmost respect for their people. They win the war for talent because
people choose to associate with them. They treat and pay their employees well. They do everything to include them in their businesses,
not exclude them. They listen to them and accept their suggestions.
They also develop them—as people in learning organizations that
contribute value and share values. That is why they keep or retain
their people and gain their long-term love and devotion.

The most admired firms are admired in large part because of the
way they engage their employees. This engagement, after all, mirrors
the very way these companies interact and interface with their

customers, supply chains, and the world at large. Common-sense businesses comprehend that corporate reputation and brand is tied to the people in their community—working together at a stated purpose. That is how the best companies view the human side of the equation.

At Cargill, for instance (see chapter 8), the human dimension is at the heart of their corporate aspirations. See the figure we've reproduced below; it comes directly from Cargill internal documents. Notice that respect and good treatment of the people involved is more than a tagline for them—it's central to their *strategy* and the very way they do business. Below the graphic is another Cargill document, "Pragmatic Impacts of Values Management." These impacts are palpable at the company and tied to the common-sense Midwestern values that have driven the firm since its inception.

Cargill Corporate Aspirations

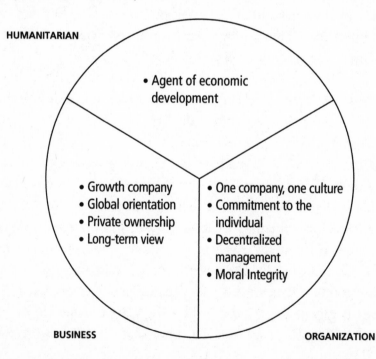

Pragmatic Impacts of Values Management

- Consistent values will attract the type of people who genuinely want to work for the company.
- Mutually held values create the trust necessary for flexibility and effectiveness.
- People at distant points in the organization can be trusted to use their intuition to solve unique operational problems consistent with organization purposes and values.
- Value-energized people will consciously seek new opportunities to fulfill these values and will not waste time on ideas that do not.
- Commonly held values tend to minimize squabbles, decrease internal frictions, and reduce time needed to manage them.
- Trust, created by similar values, allows efficient delegation. People will work independently toward commonly held goals.
- People work harder to fulfill values they believe in. This enhances personal motivation and institutional productivity.
- People sharing common values will help each other, generating teamwork and adding value through shared solutions.
- Creative people can work effectively on their own toward commonly held goals and can share the long-time horizons needed for innovative success.
- Common values create group identity, improve morale, and eliminate needs for more detailed controls.

All of this results in a set of organizational capabilities where the focus is not on structures but on the *mind-sets* that drive real behavior for both individuals and teams. Cargill achieves its success in large part due to the people, who are both highly valued themselves and who highly value the priorities that Cargill represents.

Cargill is not unlike other highly admired companies, such as office-furniture maker Herman Miller, a publicly listed company that revolves around the virtue of respect for its people, the environment, and its customers.

People Development: Setting the Tone at the Top

Fortune has named Herman Miller among its "100 Best Companies to Work For" on five separate occasions, a distinction confirmed by a host of other third-party recognitions the company has received. But what are the combination of factors that render this company's culture desirable for many of its employees, while many other American workers report feeling indifferent or even negative toward their employers?

During the financial crisis, Herman Miller CEO Brian Walker announced that he, along with four other top executives, would be taking a 10 percent pay cut in response to the economic downturn. The cut was the second one that Walker had taken, having announced a previous 10 percent cut just months prior. Accordingly, Walker would be earning a base salary of $583,000, down from the original figure of $720,000. In addition, his long-term bonus cap was adjusted to $658,790, from its original $1.62 million.

Analysts disagreed about the extent to which such a move would influence the corporate climate within the company, asking whether line employees would perceive such a move as a pro-employee gesture, or instead focus on the absolute level of the CEO pay. Nonetheless, the move received a good deal of coverage in the business press, particularly as the scrutiny over executive pay reached a boiling point in the wake of US bank failures and the global economic crisis.

Most importantly, however, the pay cut was not an isolated action. It was indicative of a larger emphasis on honoring the people of the company. The human resources group within Herman Miller places intensive focus on promoting the growth and development of individual employees. Leadership at all levels is not only allowed but encouraged: "We try to create a culture at Herman Miller where employees can be more than just their job title," said Tony Cortese, senior vice president of what they call People Services. "This is one of the few places I know of today where irrespective of your job title, you can become involved in so many different things."

Human-resource managers at the company view every worker as an "employee-owner," someone expected to take charge and be accountable for individual growth and corporate performance. The company's long-standing employee stock-ownership program, implemented in 1983, gives employees an economic stake in the company and stands as an emblem of their commitment to their people.

Why do companies like Cargill and Herman Miller get it right when so many others fail to do so? What distinguishes them from the disappointing majority? It is their approach to their employees. Their success as managers is rooted in an age-old dictum: treat others as you would want to be treated. It used to be called the Golden Rule. Today we could call it common sense.

PART II:
COMMON SENSE GLOBALLY

CHAPTER **10**
COMMON SENSE
AROUND THE WORLD

Common sense in an uncommon degree is what the world calls wisdom.

—Samuel Taylor Coleridge

Common-Sense Investing in Norway

We all have a beatific, perhaps overly romanticized picture in our minds of Norway and its scenic fjord-lined coast—either from tourist brochures or, if we are lucky, personal experience. What we are able to tell you here will not disturb any of those dreamy images; it will rather reinforce them.

Norway is a relatively small country of 5.1 million homogenous people living on a huge land terrain (149,000 square miles) stretching all the way up past the frozen Arctic Circle. But did you know that Norway has the largest Sovereign Wealth Fund (SWF) in the world? Or that it has been ranked as the number one investor in the world—since 2011? Were you aware that Norway is now viewed as the prime example for investors around the globe—as the very benchmark for both performance and professionalism?

The model of Norway's SWF is compelling precisely because of its attention to responsible behavior. This distinguishes it from almost all other SWFs. Norway's excellence comes down to one thing—its long-term time horizon. This SWF is serious about the management of wealth and has gained a reputation for structure, governance, transparency, and now especially, responsible investing. It takes all of these matters very seriously, not as afterthoughts but as core priorities. That is not to say that the Norwegian SWF is without turmoil—it is certainly scrutinized very closely—but it is to say that it does what it portends to do and has achieved an admirable record. In that sense, it is a paragon of what we are documenting in this book, namely, common-sense business. How does Norway do it? The country, of course, got to be one of the richest in the world because of its vast natural resources—fishing, hydropower, and oil and gas production. Norway is, in fact, presently the sixth largest oil-exporting country and the fifth largest gas producer in the world. Their SWF—officially named the Government Pension Fund Global (GPFG)—doesn't take this for granted and views its portfolio as the "national endowment." Seen as both a savings vehicle and a national treasure, the SWF is diversified into a broad portfolio of international securities with an ethical obligation. Commonly referred to as "The Oil Fund," or in Norwegian, *Oljefondet*, it was devised in 1998 to "insulate the domestic economy" from the resource issue—the dreaded Dutch disease—that afflicts so many resource-rich countries. This is when a sudden wealth of resources in a country leads to deindustrialization. The SWF was created to abate that occurrence in Norway, and it has worked. The total size of the SWF today is just short of one trillion dollars.

With a rigorous focus on asset allocation, allowing for little deviation, the SWF pegs to beta returns, not alpha. This lowers risk and helps long-term growth. The understanding of risk-reward is therefore different from other models or other typical funds. The SWF allows for equity across asset classes of 60 percent of the total fund.

Assets in the GPFG are not earmarked for any specific purpose, and no one has a claim on them. Transfers are not part of the state budget and accrue only to the benefit of the entire Norwegian economy and population. It was instituted from the outset so that withdrawals from the fund are anticipated as long-term annualized real returns of just 4 percent. Moderate (and limited) risks are seen as acceptable, and the overall investment strategy is ruled by ministerial decision with Parliamentary instruction, in a very open and transparent process.

This long-term, prudent strategy tilts Norway's SWF toward what is often termed "patient capital" (we talked some about this in chapter 3), liquidity-supplying and market-stabilizing value strategies. This is not a reckless, get-rich-quick scheme, and it is most certainly not a highly leveraged, big bet, casino-style capitalism. It is quite the opposite. Responsible investing is at the core of this investment brief. Holding more than 8,400 companies worldwide and more than 8,000 bonds, the SWF has since 2008 diversified further, including a 5 percent commitment for real estate. Diversity is seen as strength and a commonsensical form of rationality. With exceptionally low active management costs, the SWF demonstrates that this can be done and on a large scale.

Norway's shared ethical values are central to its success. The framework focuses on high return for future generations and respect for fundamental rights. Since the GPFG is owned ultimately by the Norwegian citizens and they cannot withdraw from investments in protest like typical shareholders can, a code of ethics was adopted to legitimize the fund. These strict guidelines exclude many companies and even entire industries. For instance, companies associated with producing certain weapons—or that even do business with countries that invest in this weaponry—can be excluded. As are companies that produce tobacco in any form, emit too much greenhouse gas, use too much coal, or engage in forced or child labor. These aren't the personal convictions of an ideological CEO, mind you. This is spelled out in their government documentation.

Hence, the GPFG avoids investments in companies whose practices constitute an unacceptable risk because of grossly unethical activities. The ethics guidelines are based on the view that there is a link between sustainable economic development and sustainable social and environmental development. The idea is that the fund, being a long-term investor, will benefit from companies respecting fundamental ethical norms based upon internationally recognized standards, such as the UN Compact and the OECD Guidelines for Multinational Enterprises.

The GPFG also posits strong positive actions as essential, such as shareholder rights, board responsibilities, well-functioning markets, climate change, water management, and children's rights. And it monitors them. This biases the selection of investments toward responsible companies and fixed instruments.

By supporting ethics in the context of performance, the Norwegian SWF has proven to be somewhat volatile, but its performance over time is favorable in terms of absolute returns over a ten-year time horizon.

Simply put, this *is* the world's best-managed fund. Could it be a bellwether for other such SWF funds? For other funds? For all investment? For pensions? For responsible, common-sense business? Yes, it is a sizeable and real demonstration project that is not only laudable but also replicable.

Common-Sense Banking in Canada

Of the group of eight highly industrialized nations (called the G8: France, Germany, Italy, the United Kingdom, Japan, the United States, Canada, and Russia), Canada is the only one that did not undergo a bank bailout during the worldwide economic recession. In fact, the top five banks in Canada—Royal Bank of Canada, Toronto Dominion, Canadian Imperial Bank of Commerce, Bank of Montreal, and Bank of Nova Scotia—dominate the list of the world's strongest banks, each with assets over $100 billion.

Now, Canadian financial institutions were hit by the same recession that everyone else suffered. Unlike most others, however, they weathered it well. Not a single institution was excessively impacted by toxic assets. No public funds were spent or injected into the system to rescue it. Instead, the banks remained profitable and continued to pay dividends. Most importantly perhaps, they continued to lend.

The Canadian policies on financial life are moderate, prudent, and unwelcoming to sophisticated products or fancy, engineered innovations—the very things that have swept and destroyed so many other balance sheets. In other words, they are based in common sense.

On regulation, Canada has an integrated regulatory approach to banks, insurance companies, and investment dealers. The banking sector is very concentrated in Canada and also highly regulated. They can engage in securities markets and in insurance, but only if the banks are offering these services though organizations that are separate and distinct from the rest of the bank. The Canadian regulatory approach is prescriptive and principles-based. It puts the onus on each firm to assure itself and to meet high national standards. So even with wise regulatory systems, Canada's *first* line of defense is at the level of the firm. This underscores the necessity of good governance structures, procedures, and corporate values, which Canada has in spades.

On balance sheets, Canadian banks are considerably less highly leveraged than their peers. Regulatory caps at asset-to-capital ratios of 20-to-1 are very different than the average in the United States and Europe, where 30-to-1 or in some cases, 40-to-1 or more (such as at Lehman Brothers) was the rule.

The key asset class that fueled the financial crisis was of course, subprime mortgages. In Canada, banks themselves hold and originate mortgages. Mortgages are not tax deductible and are viewed as long-term commitments. This incentivizes Canadian banks not to lend where there is high risk of default. Canada also has more stringent credit-worthiness and demands insurance schemes for most mortgages. There is no Fannie Mae or Freddie Mac in Canada pumping the mortgage system with public money. Interest deductions are not tax deductible, and lending is much more conservative generally, and with more recourse. All this meant that in Canada, there was no housing bubble in the first place, so there was nothing fragile to burst.

Because of the contribution of sound macroeconomic management, regulatory systems, corporate governance structures, and banking parameters, Canada has produced the soundest financial sector in the world according to the World Economic Forum. Capital requirements for Canadian banks are above average by international standards. They also rely more on depository funds than on wholesale funding.

What lessons can be drawn? Prudent long-term fiscal and monetary policies impact positively any given financial sector. In this case, Canada was well served. Globalization has brought with it a level of interconnectedness among markets that can make your head spin. We have to get the basics of regulation right so as to avoid arbitrage and maintain currency values and competitiveness. Again, Canada deserves high marks here for keeping the long term in view. Some may think such common-sense banking to be boring, but it paid off when the chips were down.

Systematic risk and moral hazard are an issue for any nation. "Too big to fail" is a very expensive, politicized way to rescue institutions. Transparency is critical, and taking on less risk and understanding those risks is a good place to start. Canada knew and did all this.

So, can Toronto teach New York, London, and the world anything (as the headlines read)?[1] Yes, it can. Stability is something to invest in. Obviously, Canadian history and context sets it apart from all other countries, but Canada's banks are more strictly regulated, more fully tested, show more restraint on risky banking behavior and activities, and thereby prevent crises.

The real bottom line is that conventional wisdom shows a better way in Canada. That prudent way of common sense involves rational procedures, risk management, and more stable practices. It results in more successful outcomes over a whole cycle and especially during a bubble or a far-reaching financial crisis. Oh, Canada!

Common-Sense Small Business in Britain

Strolling down "high street" (what Americans might call "main street") in just about any town in Great Britain, you see all the same familiar shops, stores, establishments, and banks, all in a row. What many of us don't comprehend is how many of them have survived a long time and originated from various nonconformist—Quaker, Methodist, and Catholic—spiritual traditions. What sets these firms apart? And why did they come about in the first place? Is high street in Britain going to last, or will it too fade away under new pressures?

High street is of course, as the name suggests, the main commercial and retail street in a given town. In most big cities in the UK, each neighborhood has its own high street. The idea originated in the Middle Ages, where the notion of "high" described an order of ranking. Over time, high street has lost that definition and simply has come to mean the place where banks and shops locate to do everyday retail business. High street probably came to its zenith around the 1870s because of increased urbanization in Britain. These shops, with fixed prices, good customer service, and home delivery, quickly took off. In Edwardian England, the suffragettes wanted somewhere respectable to go, and such high streets offered just that. The stores were clean, well-tended, honest, and stocked with goods of high and reliable quality. They made business common sense.

Today, many high streets have suffered and are in need of reinvention. Quaint and valuable shops are closing, people are moving to the suburbs, online retailers are making greater inroads, and big-box stores are luring people away from good ol' high street. What companies do we witness disappearing? They include the likes of Boots, the chemists, Barclays Bank, WHSmith, the booksellers, Cadbury (until it was sold off), Marks & Spencer, The Co-op Group, John Lewis, H&M, C&A, Debenhams, Thorntons, and the list goes on and on.

Britain is taking notice, so hopefully, high street won't die quietly and maybe will even revive. Rejuvenation would bring shoppers back and make cities and neighborhoods more attractive—as well as commercially viable—again. The House of Commons and a number of commissions and reports have raised awareness among Parliament and the general public about a range of issues impacting small shopkeepers, who have been disappearing from High Street each year at rather alarming rates.

A recent Deloitte consumer report entitled "Reinventing the Role of the High Street" provides lots of statistics about how high streets have fallen into demise for more than a decade. The issues identified are oversupply, affordability, purpose, changing focus and behaviors, and digital acceleration. Another report, High Street UK 2020 Project Report, by the Institute of Place Management, spells out a gloomy picture of companies failing, stores closing, and a decline in the number of employees in high street establishments. Then there is "The Portas Review: An Independent Review into the Future of our High Streets," which provided an independent review on the status and future of high street, including ideas for reinvigoration.

Whether High Street survives, is reinvented, or simply muddles though is still undetermined. But it is worth asking serious and deeper questions about the past to color the future. Why did nonconformist companies, rooted in honesty and providing customer-driven products and services, thrive for so long on high street? What is it about the way they did business that was so laudable and valued—and sustainable for hundreds of years? Most importantly, can there be a new high street for a new era—one that gets right what the original one got right *and* avoids the pitfalls of inhumane economic growth?

Common-Sense Tea Legacies in Japan

The oldest company in Japan is a temple builder named Kongo Gumi, founded in the year 578. But not much younger are a number of Japanese tea companies. Now anyone who has experienced a Japanese tea ceremony (*chanoyu* in Japanese, which translates as "hot water") realizes how seriously the Japanese take their tea. Tea came to Japan from China many centuries ago, along with the Zen Buddhist philosophy. Drinking tea remains a spiritual exercise in Japan; it embodies harmony, respect, and purity, and it provides a deep sense of tranquility. It is a deeply spiritual and communal experience to be enjoyed and savored. Sipping tea during the traditional tea ceremony takes hours and is to be used as a period for reflection and to experience real satisfaction.

Ippodo Tea Company, located in Kyoto, has made tea for about 1,500 years. Not just a retailer, the company is involved in tea procurement and blending, selecting only the finest leaves. These leaves are carefully cultivated in the fields surrounding the region, which is particularly renown for producing the highest grade of tea in Japan, if not the world. Thanks to its mild, misty climate, mineral-rich soil, and perfect balance of sunshine and rain, the area is particularly well suited for growing tea.

Ippodo tea doesn't come cheap. For as we discovered on our visit to the company, there are no shortcuts. The range of teas at Ippodo includes sencha, known for its balance between sweetness and sharpness; bancha, an everyday casual tea with low caffeine; and matcha, the classic powdered green tea that is whisked into its pea-green color by infusion.

The small town of Uji is at the heart of the tea business and has been for a very long time. It is located between Kyoto and the ancient capital of Nara, about 230 miles southwest of Tokyo. The tea here grows in the natural contours of the hills and valleys in straight, tightly trimmed rows that look more like ornamental hedges than bushes.

A co-operative called Nagata runs the small, manicured plantations, and they source their organic teas to the Ippodo Company. Rejecting chemical spraying completely, they do not use animal manures, chemical fertilizers, herbicides, or any pesticides. They use vegetable-quality compost. They keep to nature and stress the importance of building and keeping the soil vitality. Their plants suffer less blight and mold and typically produce tea leaves for over forty years, and some as long as one hundred years. This is easily twice as long as other tea producers who treat with chemicals.

The company, as are most Japanese, is well aware of the legendary health benefits of green tea. When we visited, we had the opportunity to enjoy a matcha green tea and make it ourselves (with instruction). We met the owners and managers of Ippodo, who shared their story and common-sense, long-term business philosophy with us. Besides an amazing cup of tea, we took away these principles:

First, the company is extraordinarily sensitive to its environment. They strive to remain in harmony with the world around them. They know what they are part of and the ecosystem in which they participate. They also have strong ties to the community and to the larger Japanese society.

Secondly, they are cohesive. A strong identity gives them a sense of belonging to something very old and dear. They realize their achievements. Strong employee links provide an endearing notion of community. The managers are chosen from within the company. Generations of employees give the company a feeling of being part of a family. They are members in a co-operative enterprise. As stewards of a tradition, they grasp the part they play in a long—in this case, very long—chain. The primary concern is with the health of the enterprise as a whole.

Third, they are tolerant. The processes are quite decentralized. They remain open to experiment even though they have total quality control. They seek to stretch their possibilities constantly.

And fourth, they are very conservative, especially when it comes to finance. Frugal would be the operative word, with little risk taking. As old fashioned as you can be, the company believes money gives them flexibility and independence of action. To put it another way, they value their own freedom to do what is prudent for their business. And they don't get too caught up in financial reports. They say figures describe the past, and they are constantly looking to the future.

With no worry about ROI for shareholders, profitability is gauged over a long term. The company actually confessed to having a 150-year strategic plan! Ha! They definitely plan to stay in business!

Best-selling author Jim Collins found some of the same traits in his classic studies of companies that were "built to last."[2] These companies change and adapt without compromising cherished core ideals.

As a living company, this Japanese tea company has survived and thrived by focusing on the long run and on their own values. Prudence, prudence, prudence....or as the Japanese would say, *Chui, chui, chui.*

Common-Sense Technology Business in India

If ever you are lost, you can find your way back by setting your gaze on the powerful Polaris, or "north star." The Indian financial technology company by the same name is similarly guided.

Claiming to run on "the power of intellect," Polaris was founded in 1993 and has become a global leader in financial technology for banking, insurance, and other financial services. Headquartered in Chennai, the company has a clear purpose statement: "By nurturing sharp, deep understanding of the life cycle of money in the lives of individuals, communities, banks, and financial institutions, it simplifies and makes technology work for businesses with a personal touch."

Across the Americas, Europe, Middle East, Asia-Pacific, and Australia and New Zealand, Polaris has a broad reach. It has corporate online banking in 120 countries, trade financing in eighty-one countries, payment services in fifty-three countries, treasury solutions in twenty-three countries, and ATM solutions on three continents. It is actively seeking new customers on every continent daily, yet 96 percent of its customers are repeat customers. This number says a *lot* for long-term stability.

Polaris is a company that has gone "from smart to wise," to use the vernacular. Because even brilliant technicians can make foolish mistakes if they depart from common sense. Polaris has stayed on track by sticking to its original core values. These are hard-baked into the company and have been since its founder, Arun Jain, started it.

Now this is a technology services and product company—make no mistake about it—the kind India has become synonymous with. It offers a full spectrum of offerings: testing, infrastructure management, business efficiency, business transformation, data and analytics, mobility and channels, and risk and compliance. Its systems run in over 250 financial institutions worldwide. But that doesn't mean that Polaris isn't about more than profits. Polaris benefits its clients, its employees, and the planet over the long term.

It achieves this by nurturing a high-performance, sustainable work culture rooted in spiritual capital. It sets out to be a people-oriented enterprise where leadership is not thwarted but rewarded. There is a real spirit of ownership for the employees, all of whom own stock in the company. Collaboration is valued as a strength and is embraced as part of the company's own process of ongoing learning. Polaris invented Lakshya, a free-flowing open-space platform to explore the organization's direction without loading it down with current constraints. Their annual Lakshya conference builds what they term "subconscious thinking"; it uncovers new paths and opportunities. It also helps them discover suboptimal "I didn't know what I didn't know" zones. This is importantly a bottom-up, experiential forum of discovery—not a top-down drill.

Polaris has a strong code of conduct; they train on it incessantly. And ethics is at the core of their business—from the board level to the lowest employee in the firm. They focus on six dimensions of value: customer capital, human capital, execution capital, intellectual property capital, brand capital, and finance capital. Such an integrated model is exceptional among global companies and grows out of Polaris's Indian spiritual values and traditions, which are in fact quite cosmopolitan and relevant in our global age.

Polaris has serious commitments to environmental protection and not only continuously improves their compliance in that space but works to ensure energy and resource conservation. Their goal is to minimize any damage caused to the natural environment. When it comes to corporate social responsibility, Polaris is not just interested in charity and philanthropic activity. It goes much further in supporting social, economic, and ethical responsibility by embedding it in the organizational culture as a way to develop the society around it.

So the company creates support systems for families and actively seeks to integrate the firm into the larger community.

One specific way it does this is the Ullas Trust (ullastrust.org). Started by employees to integrate Polaris with the larger Indian community, it recognizes academic excellence in adolescent students from the most economically challenged sections of society. These students are encouraged through mentoring, scholarships, workshops, coaching, and exposure to the corporate environment to pursue and achieve their education potential.

Another award-winning program is called SAMPADA (Special Appreciation and Mentoring Program Acknowledging Differently Abled), which advocates for and creates opportunities for the talented, disabled professional. SAMPADA means ramp access to all areas of the workplace and wheelchair-friendly bathrooms, cafeterias, and offices; specially trained facilitators; and warm, patient interactions at work. Employees sourcing from SAMPADA can qualify for free housing close to work as well as special commuting facilities. The results have been amazing and encouraging, and now 18 percent of Polaris employees come to the company through SAMPADA.

This kind of "community development" is more than just marching in parades and sponsoring little-league teams. It is building up the company with loyal, quality employees within a culture of respect and responsibility. In a location with little government support for the disabled person or the underprivileged student scholar (compared to what we may be used to), Polaris is making a deep and meaningful difference.

So there's no question that on the Virtue Matrix (chapter 6), Polaris ventures boldly out into the frontier, but does it do it at the cost of profits and market share? The results speak for themselves. With more than 12,500 employee experts and the world's foremost and first design center for financial services, Polaris is a path-breaking company with laser-like focus. Today, Polaris is the chosen partner of nine of the top ten banks and seven of the top ten global insurance companies. Their business model is working. In fact, it is dominating.

Citibank may have helped to start Polaris and it may still be its largest client, but the company is now a true global entity. Awarded India's best CSR (corporate social responsibility) company by NASS-COM (a public policy group for the Indian software industry), Polaris was also selected to the *Forbes* list of best companies in the world under $1 billion. This high energy, highly professional, fiercely ethical, globally respected company, revolves around the two themes of *quality* and *relationships.* The leadership at Polaris balances functional and intelligent systems in an Eastern way that has a very noble purpose. It is authentic. It knows when and how to lead. It makes decisions based on discernment and isn't afraid of major changes (at the advice of BCG consultants, Polaris divided its business into two companies in 2014). But foremost, Polaris cultivates enlightened long-term self-interest. These traits taken together make it a common-sense business model from which we all can profitably learn.

Common-Sense Small Enterprise in Germany

It was only in 2009 that Germany—populated by roughly 80 million people—had to pass on the position of global-export champion to China—a country of far more than a billion. Germany had long held the position, demonstrating the enormous success of its products in the globalized markets of the twenty-first century.

There are more than 1,500 German "global market leaders" (companies holding position 1–3 in global turnover at the branch level). If asked to name a few, many people would think first about Volkswagen and Daimler, SAP and Siemens. However, the field is much more rich than that. More than 35 percent of German exports stem from roughly 3,000 small- and medium-sized enterprises (SMEs). These SMEs each have only 50–250 employees and a turnover between €50 million and €1 billion. Many of these companies are very successful economically and realize a higher return on capital employed than stock-listed blue-chip companies! Most are privately held, family-based firms. Some have graduated to become major global players over the years. Taken together, they are known in Germany as the *Mittelstand*.

The *Mittelstand* is "the backbone of the German economy," according to the German Chamber of Commerce. Unbelievably, 99 percent of German companies are SMEs. That's 3.6 million companies and over 60 percent of the entire workforce. Not only are 95 percent of these companies still family owned, but 85 percent of them are still managed by their owners. The term of a CEO is less of a career and more of a dynasty! The *average* CEO in a *Mittelstand* company stays twenty years.

It is noticeable from the beginning that these "wunderkind" companies are not typically located in major city centers but rather in (sometimes remote) regional towns in the Black Forest, the Bergisches Land, the Swabian Alp, the Sauerland, Eastern Westphalia, Bavaria, and in rural Franconia. They cross almost every industry sector and line of business, including mechanical engineering, plant construction, automotive industry, advanced manufacturing, and tool making.

These companies have highly specialized products with global distribution and a global leader's position in their particular markets. Their comfortable competitive position, however, often contrasts with low public visibility even in their own geographical backyard—a combination that stimulates many to refer to them as "hidden champions." Both economic success as well as modest public perception are, of course, rooted in the character of these humble owner-entrepreneurs, who are very industrious and smart business people but who also avoid public relations and prefer more than just a glossy appearance. They are essentially common-sense business people who have sustained themselves and their companies for long periods of time. What lies behind their success? A principled business culture based on time-tested values.

The vast majority of these German SME entrepreneurs of the *Mittelstand* have been raised with clear Christian values, which firmly link faith in God with a sense of personal responsibility, self-discipline, hard work, and engagement for and with other people. This culture is nurtured in a parish but more importantly within the entrepreneurial family itself, and often over numerous generations. Prudence—the first (and weightiest) part of common-sense business—is in their DNA.

Family and Meaningful Work

These German entrepreneurs know very well that it is difficult for them to compete with larger multinationals, which can offer far better fringe benefits and higher public esteem, not to mention higher salaries. Therefore, many of the *Mittelstand* companies invest strongly in a family-centric culture, which combines competitive payment with an early and high degree of responsibility, a strong sense of belonging, and very meaningful work. In their situation, not only is this kind of investment in line with their values, it's only common sense. Meaningful work produces goods and services that truly improve life. Thus, their employees strongly identify with their occupation and view their own contribution as a vocation and not merely a job.

Many aspects emphasized by the "servant leadership" theory of management are crucial for these *Mittelstand* companies. Only if employees are empowered to develop their personal capabilities and to grow as persons can the long-term value of the companies be augmented. In such durable settings, finance comes second to responsibility and solid workmanship that people can be proud of.

Since employees are not recognized as an exchangeable workforce but rather as persons of dignity, uniqueness, and true worth, they are considered co-creators of the business success. A strong and collaborative business culture is of upmost importance for the high quality standards required in many technical production processes of *Mittelstand* companies. So if you ask these German SME entrepreneurs about their values and responsibilities, their first thought goes not to their mission statement or financial reports but to their people. The human element is paramount. That's one reason these companies stay in their smaller towns rather than transferring to big cities. Doing so enables staffers to work close to their homes and extended families, to avoid stressful commutes, and to make a living in an area where housing prices are reasonable and natural beauty abounds.

Little impressed by much-touted concepts like "corporate social responsibility" and "corporate citizenship," these German entrepreneurs go in fact far beyond what those trendy labels denote. As a matter of course, they are champions of engagement within their local environments and give back to their communities. They support the regional soccer clubs, cooperate with local schools, and frequently hold positions in the local chambers of commerce and in their churches and voluntary associations. What is more, they are above-average apprenticing companies and contribute to the important fact that youth unemployment in Germany is still among the lowest in all of Europe.

Values and Cooperation

Mittelstand entrepreneurs in general nurture reservations against all kinds of institutions. First and foremost, they are concerned about union influence. They put more trust in codetermination—a very old, firm-level idea involving organized worker's councils (*Betriebsräte*). Many of the *Mittelstand* companies operate under what has been called a values management system (VMS). The idea is the result of cooperative thinking between the Centre for Business Ethics, the German Network for Business Ethics, and a vast array of firms and economic associations.

The VMS is dynamic and aims to guide the implementation and evaluation of good management practices. The overriding aim of the VMS is a company's sustainable stabilization in every sense (legal, economic, ecological, and social). Put simply, it is all about building common sense into businesses.

Based on the corporate culture described above, *Mittelstand* entrepreneurs are in favor of an active dialogue with their own personnel. Many *Betriebsräte* are serving as credible mediators and contribute hugely to the successful development of their companies. This could change, however, as worker representatives become the local organ of centralized (and sometimes ideologically orientated) union organizations. In such a setting, representatives are not merely interested in the companies' sustainable success but rather in fostering their own careers inside of the union by promoting "politically correct" issues and ideological positions.

Independence

Mittelstand German entrepreneurs often are critical of the media and of the public sector. If possible, they also tend to stay independent of banks and most outside capital. The reason is certainly not a generalized distrust; they wouldn't be supporters of trust-based relations if it were—they would never be so successful on global markets, either. Rather, these German entrepreneurs sense by intuition that dependence on external forces would endanger their genuine values-based business culture. Acting against one's own convictions to serve external guidelines would threaten the credibility of their sense of responsibility and darken the visibility of the value base for one's employees.

The *Mittelstand* is therefore a key element of German civil society—sometimes even to a larger extent than NGOs, which are financially dependent on public sponsorship. The German "economic miracle" would not have started or continued so long without these companies that are so critical to the German economy and so prudent in the ways of work. They are deeply inspired by their traditions and have introduced economic, managerial, and institutional innovations that have stood up over time under the pressure of competing in a global economy.

Together they have also influenced the larger German economic order of *soziale marktwirtschaft,* or social market economy. A kind of third way apart from pure capitalism and pure social-welfare, it combines what its supporters believe to be the best of both. This national law originated with a Catholic priest who became minister of labor after World War II, and it has been important to the development of a cooperative business culture in Germany ever since.

Let's look at a few examples of these *Mittelstand* companies (as typical of the entire grouping) to get an idea of their strengths, since they cross all sectors and industries and have come to define German productivity.

Four Mittelstand Companies

DM is a company that operates drug stores across Germany and in Eastern Europe. Founded in 1977, it is based in Karlsruhe. It remains privately held by its founder, Professor Gotz Werner. It is heralded as the leading retailer in its highly competitive field. DM has a very low turnover rate. Employees value the work atmosphere that gives them an unusual degree of autonomy. They are also paid way above average. The firm's founder abhors the idea that people would work for him just to take home pay. And so he does everything to create a corporate culture around respect and appreciation. His ideal is that, even if all his workers were to receive an unconditional government-supplied basic income (an idea that he favors, by the way!), they'd stay simply because they enjoy and thrive on the interactions with their colleagues and customers.

Vaude is a textile company that focuses on mountain-sports equipment. Headquartered in Teitnang, it has 1,600 employees and is growing rapidly. It was founded in 1974 by Albrecht von Dewitz, and he remains its CEO. The company is acquiring and opening more stores and invests its profits into that strategy. It is also considered at the forefront of logistics, as it has developed a logistics center that is the envy of all its competitors. Today, the founder's daughter runs the firm as COO. Vaude is 100 percent family owned, and 60 percent of its sales are generated in Germany. It is a leader in recycling and maintains strong sustainability policies using the stringent Bluesign for their environmental standards. As a member of the multi-stakeholder organization Fair Wear, Vaude is at the forefront of global product design.

Westaflex makes auto parts. It has been family owned since its founding in 1901. Supplying the automobile industry for nearly 125 years, the company has two divisions: convertible roofs; and heating, cooling, and ventilation. With sales of €2.4 billion, it now has more than 10,000 employees and fifty locations all over the world. The company is considered a world leader in innovation and technology. It started as a *Mittelstand* company and keeps those values.

Miele is a well-known appliance company that has graduated into a rather large multinational but had its start in the *Mittelstand*. (We talk much more about this company in the next chapter.) It makes high-end domestic appliances and in 2007 was voted the most successful company in Germany. Miele is indeed a poster child for the success of the *Mittelstand* model.

Secrets of the Mittelstand

In summary, the focus of *Mittelstand* companies is rather different from that of many corporations. Great value is placed on lasting relationships with customers, suppliers, employees, and stakeholders, and quality and innovation, not pricing, is paramount. These entities highly value collaboration. They prize their employees and have remained, even under considerable pressure, small and family oriented. They are modern and cosmopolitan, yet they invest more than do typical companies to create new jobs. With a view that they are here to stay, they build social responsibility into the very way they operate and integrate it into their strategy at every turn. As customer-centric firms, the *Mittelstand* worship their customers. They get as close to them as possible. Indeed, many of the products they sell require customization, even ongoing consultation, which cements this customer orientation. They follow Peter Drucker's sage dictum: "The purpose of business is to create and keep a customer."

The Institute for Mittelstand Research, located in Bonn, has shown how truly global these "local" companies are. They tend to sell direct, rather than through joint ventures, and the SME sector is responsible for 70 percent of all German exports. Hermann Simon, a German management expert who has studied the *Mittelstand* for decades, decoded their core principles in his book *Hidden Champions of the 21st Century: Success Strategies of Unknown World Market Leaders.*[3] His foremost finding was that these companies succeed by what he called "constant innovation." They may have narrow business segments, but they specialize so as to become "sons of niches." Sticking to their core competencies, they are extremely patient and follow strict risk-mitigation strategies and protocols.

The *Mittelstand* companies have oriented their businesses in prudent, sustainable, common-sense fashion. They see themselves as responsible not just for the firm but for the people they support and on whom they depend—and especially for the communities where they reside and work. We can benefit a lot from their example.

NOTES

1. For instance, Chrystia Freeland, "What Toronto Can Teach New York and London," *Financial Times* (January 29, 2010): www.ft.com.
2. Jim Collins, *Built to Last: Successful Habits of Visionary Companies* (HarperBusiness, 1994).
3. (Springer, 2009).

CHAPTER 11
MIELE: SURVIVING AND THRIVING

Recently, we were sitting in the traditional Swabian town of Gütersloh in southern Germany, talking with the family scions of one of the nation's leading companies. It has grown from its *Mittelstand* roots (see chapter 10) to become a truly global player.

Peering out the window of Miele's modern, unpretentious offices, two things become apparent. First, this is a modern, sustainable company focused on its global future and fashioned around a single word: *innovation*. But it is also in many ways, like the town it inhabits, a very old fashioned, traditional company of demonstrable values that many of its peers have jettisoned; it knows and practices common-sense business.

The Miele Company has a long and rich history of quality engineering. *Immer Besser* or "Forever Better" was established early as the company motto, and it stands for a commitment to the highest quality standards, longevity, and improvement—both in production and in business practices. As our conversation with the family owners demonstrated, they sincerely believe in these things. The embodiment of this philosophy is as relevant today as it was over 125 years ago. Things may move ahead at a record pace but here, at Miele, they also stand still—and are unwavering: they employ common sense in their strategy and their execution of business plans, which are focused over a very long term.

Founded in 1899 by a farmer's son, Carl Miele, and a salesman, Reinhard Zinkann, The Miele Company remains independently owned and managed by the Miele and Zinkann families. With global headquarters in small, rural Gütersloh, Miele is nevertheless a world leader in the production of premium domestic and commercial appliances. There are eight production plants in Germany and also plants in Austria, the Czech Republic, Romania, and China. Miele has its own wholly owned sales subsidiaries in forty-seven countries now and is represented in a further forty-eight by distribution partners. Company turnover exceeds €4 billion.

The case we will explore shows *why* and *how* Miele grew into what it has become and it also underscores how its closely held common-sense values undergird everything it stands for and does. New and old are *one* here.

History of Miele[1]
Immer Besser Begins

In 1899, Carl Miele and Reinhard Zinkann founded Miele & Cie. KG in Herzebrock, a German town that is now in the modern state of North Rhine-Westphalia. Miele had agricultural roots, and their first product was a cream separator used by farmers to produce cream from milk. Their beginnings were humble: There were eleven workers, and they only had four lathes and one drill. Gradually, in 1901, the company expanded its product line by making Meteor butter churns, which liberated local farming ladies from hand churning.

However, Miele soon seized upon a great opportunity for problem solving that would underpin its dramatic growth. In the early twentieth century, doing laundry was arduous and could take several days to do well. Dirty laundry was soaked overnight and subjected to tough rubbing by hand to remove stains, before being hurled into a large tub where it had to be cooked in hot water and stirred by a paddle.

To reduce this backbreaking workload, Miele released its first washing machine, the Hera. Working this machine still required much human labor, since it had paddles that needed to be moved, using a crank or lever. However, this machine made life better for its users, and so it proved to be very popular.

Miele constantly improved its cream separators, butter churns, and washing machines. With the increasing use of electricity in cities, the first electric cream separator appeared in 1910, followed by the first electric washing machine a year later. As waterpower was still cheaper and more readily available than electricity, Miele built a water-powered washing machine in 1914. By 1926, Miele was selling twenty-four models of washing machines, catering to different kinds of customers.

New products rapidly appeared: motorcars (1912), bicycles (1924), milking machines (1926), vacuum cleaners (1927), electric irons (1928), dishwashers (1929), ice boxes (1932), and motorcycles (1933). Not all of Miele's ventures were successful. In the 1910s, the automobile industry was growing fast, and Miele was one of many companies seeking to grab a share of that market. Between 1912 and 1914, 143 Miele automobiles were sold. However, Miele's management eventually decided to retreat from that business to avoid the huge capital investments needed to remain profitable.

Survival and Growth

Miele's flood of high-quality innovations helped it to survive and thrive both before and during World War I, and in the tumultuous period between the World Wars. In less than ten years, the company grew to sixty employees. In 1907, the founders moved their business to nearby Gütersloh. They bought a much larger factory for their business, with a railway link and an iron foundry, and established four regional sales offices. In 1911, the company again expanded their production facilities. These included a non-ferrous foundry and facilities for metal plating. By World War I, Miele was employing more than five hundred people.

After Germany was defeated in 1918, the German economy suffered from hyperinflation into the early 1920s. After a few years of recovery, the crash of the New York Stock Exchange triggered the Great Depression, which decimated worldwide economic activity. The founders managed to steer the company remarkably well during these dark years; they continually released a stream of new products while expanding existing businesses. By the time Zinkann and Miele died in 1938 and 1939, Miele employed 2,700 people, and about two thousand Miele products were exported to numerous countries. From just four regional offices, the company had built a vast web of warehouses, showrooms, and sales offices in Germany, Austria, Belgium, France, Poland, Argentina, and Switzerland.

World War II and the Aftermath

In 1939, the year when Nazi Germany invaded Poland, the sons of the two founders—Carl Miele, Jr. and Kurt Christian Zinkann—took over the management of Miele. For a short time, a trusted employee, C.H. Walkenhorst, who had worked with the two founders for years, guided the new managers.

World War II proved catastrophic for Miele. The company was compelled to make whatever the Nazi war machine demanded. This was a complete disruption of its primary mission to make quality appliances that improve human life. However, some production was still devoted to bicycles and wagons. In the final years of the war, Germany was scourged by waves of Allied bombers and massive invasions from both the East and the West. Miele lost many workers, and many of its assets were obliterated.

The victorious Allies carved a devastated Germany into four zones after the war. Miele, which had somehow survived, adjusted to the rudimentary needs of the survivors in what later became West Germany. Going back to its original roots, the company resumed the production of wooden tub washing machines and continued making wagons. It also built coal-fired ovens from the metal remaining in the ruins. In 1949, four years after the war had been lost, Miele's product range remained significantly narrower than before.

The Miracle Years

The Marshall Plan and the economic recovery of Europe eventually allowed a German economic miracle to begin.

Demand for appliances in reviving West Germany was exploding in the 1950s, and Miele improved its products and expanded their range. Fully automated appliances, such as a washing machine (1956) and a dishwasher (1960), were launched. The first domestic tumble-dryer was introduced in 1958. Old products such as bicycles and motorcycles reached new peaks of production.

Miele continued to innovate, incorporating microelectronics into their equipment in the 1960s and 1970s. In 1969, Miele started selling built-in kitchens—a whole kitchen armed with a range of Miele products. Meanwhile, they continued to expand the range of its products, introducing microwaves, electric ovens, stove hoods, steam cookers, and coffee makers. To free up resources for other product lines, the company stopped making bicycles and motorcycles in 1960.

The company also extended its existing product lines, manufacturing, for example, a whole range of washing machines for commercial use, including a specialized line for washing the protective suits of fire fighters. In the 1980s, the company also capitalized on its expertise for making dishwashers by manufacturing specialized machines for disinfecting surgical instruments.

In 1985, three Miele leaders, including Kurt Christian Zinkann, died. Shortly after, CEO Carl Miele, Jr. also passed away. Rudolf Miele and Peter Zinkann, grandsons of the company founders, succeeded them. The new management concentrated on international expansion, with new subsidiaries founded in Australia, South Africa, Ireland, and the United States.

German Reunification and Beyond

The Berlin Wall fell in 1989, and East and West Germany became one nation once more in 1990. After fifty years, Miele products reappeared in East Germany and were met with acclaim. Sales offices in Leipzig and Berlin were opened. Meanwhile, the company continued to expand its international presence, conquering many Eastern European and Asian markets, including Russia, Japan, Hong Kong, and Singapore.

During the 1990s, Miele's revenues continually expanded. By 1999, the company's centenary year, Miele had grossed DM3.9 billion, with 14,364 employees. Fifty-six percent of the company's revenues were coming from exports.

To keep up with this growth, the company had to continually expand production facilities and capacities. Besides organic growth, the company also made some acquisitions. In 1986, Miele acquired Cordes, a Westphalia laundry-technology specialist. Four years later, Imperial, a German manufacturer of built-in appliances, was acquired.

Unlike many of its peers, Miele generally did not shift production to cheaper locations to reduce costs. Remarkably, most of its manufacturing facilities can be reached within a day trip from company headquarters. To further maintain the highest quality standards, Miele even developed and manufactured the electronic controls used in its appliances.

More recently, the company achieved revenues of €3.2 billion (approximately DM6.31 billion), with 17,660 employees. In 2014, it had subsidiaries in forty-seven countries and had a presence in fifty more through importers. Through wars, recessions, and national devastation, Miele & Cie. KG, now under the management of the fourth-generation descendants of the founders, has come a long way while remaining true to its core Germanic tradition of innovation and quality. With the exception of the period immediately after World War II, when it had to write off the damage from the war, Miele has never reported a loss.

Quality, Innovation, Responsibility[2]

In the beginning, Carl Miele and Reinhard Zinkann marked each of their cream separators with the words, *Semper Melior* ("Always Better"), which later gave rise to Miele's forward-thinking motto mentioned earlier, *Immer Besser* ("Forever Better"). It was a promise to customers that every product from Miele is of the best quality. It was an assurance that the Miele product in their hands is superior to that of the competition in all ways. This promise applied to the Miele butter churns and wooden tub washing machines of a century ago; it applies to the coffee machines and steam cookers of today. Miele's attention to quality is fanatical. As the 2013 Miele Sustainability Report put it, "a consumer should get a product that has been optimized in every conceivable aspect." It is a product constructed with premium materials and components, and a result of years of research and development.

One manifestation of this focus is how all Miele products are constructed to last at least twenty years. Each new dishwasher model, for instance, must prove its ability to pass severe endurance assessments that simulate its use over 12,500 hours, which equates to an astonishing one million dishes washed! In addition to testing new models, tests are also performed on random appliances from existing production lines. This is followed by the 100 percent inspection of all production.

Miele also goes well beyond the legal requirements to ensure product safety. Besides intensive testing, the company is highly vertically integrated (almost 50 percent), and this allows Miele to tightly monitor the quality of key components, an important contributor to product safety. (Note that we already discussed the myriad benefits of vertical integration to a large company, in chapter 8). Miele backs this up with rigorous monitoring of complaints and returns. In the highly improbable event of a recall, elaborate contingency plans are in place for execution and review of existing processes. All these activities lead to excellent product safety, and the company states that almost all the few accidents involving Miele products are due to user errors.

Finally, Miele strives to produce products that easily beat competitors' performance. For example, among the manufacturers of commercial dishwashers, only Miele offers fresh water systems, which achieve much more hygienic results. To enhance this further, these units also offer customized washing options that feature elevated rinsing temperatures (over 93°C) and significant temperature holding times (up to ten minutes).

Although they do produce some products and parts in Austria, Romania, China, and the Czech Republic, Miele keeps most of its production close to home, allowing it to capitalize on superb German engineering and craftsmanship. This helps to ensure durability, safety, and performance. Miele is willing to accept the high wages of Germany and Europe in order to ensure the premium quality of their products. As Dr. Markus Miele, current co-owner of Miele put it, "If you make a promise, you must also keep it. Quality must be part of our everyday operation, and constantly considered from different angles."

Miele's focus on quality is inseparable from its tradition of innovation. Its motto inspires Miele's workers to continually improve their performance. It is a call to never be complacent but to make the perfect even more perfect. Miele's long history of new and better products, and the countless technical innovations that underlie them, is the best testimony to this. Dr. Reinhard Zinkann, co-owner of Miele emphasized this: "Every business must always take on new challenges; time doesn't stand still. *Tempora mutantur, nos et mutamur in illis*—the times change and we change with them."

Given the company's fanatical focus on quality and innovation, "Best model in test: Miele" is often the outcome of international product tests. Twelve Miele appliances were awarded top marks or were test winners between 2000 and 2005 in tests by Stiftung Warentest (StiWa), Germany's leading consumer association. In tests performed by *Which?*, the British Consumer Association's magazine, Miele products routinely achieve top marks. Miele vacuum cleaners in particular have received positive reviews from consumer associations around the world.

Finally, Miele's understanding of quality is inseparable from its sense of responsibility. The company aims to deliver the maximum positive impact—the best products and the optimum customer experience—but at minimum environmental cost. Thus, it boasts of products that can not only deliver the best performance, but also deliver it with stellar energy efficiency. The very durability of Miele products means that they will not be quickly thrown away, allowing natural resources to be carefully conserved. Even in the earliest years, durable oak wood was used as the base material for the wooden-tub washing machines.

Beyond product-related values, the company is committed to responsible human values. For four generations, the executive board has practiced a responsible style of corporate governance that applies to Miele's relationship with all stakeholders. Their governance style is based on mutual respect of all involved.

It is interesting how *stable* the company's commitment is to its core common-sense values. On first glance, its governance structure would not necessarily facilitate this. Miele is governed by five executive directors who are all equal: two representatives of the Miele and Zinkann families, and three powerful non-family members. Parallel to this board, the shareholder committee represents the shareholders and comprises three representatives each from the proprietor families. Decisions need a 60 percent majority. Such a fragmented structure does not seem to promote stability.

Yet, perhaps because of the powerfully entrenched culture, there is a strong uniformity of opinion on topics such as Miele's responsibility toward customers, staff, and the environment, or the need to remain an independent family-owned business that largely funds itself. There are also clear rules that govern dividend payouts, shares transfer, and the procedure through which members of proprietor families take up jobs in the company. These are issues that often disastrously divide family-owned businesses. Not so at Miele. In fact, Miele's managing director, Dr. Rheinhard Zinkann, was part of a national commission producing the Governance Code for Family Enterprises—a guiding document for formulating sound family constitutions to guide governance. Miele's management rules and culture thus facilitate the consistent commitment to its values.

Miele can be characterized as one of the most successful of the *Mittelstand*—albeit one that can no longer claim the label, as it has been many years since it could be described as small- or medium-sized. For the past 114 years, through all the challenges and changes, the company has remained true to its core *Mittelstand* values of quality, innovation, and responsibility. It has met the demanding standards that it has set for itself and kept the promises it has made to stakeholders. It has indeed been a company committed to be "forever better."

Spiritual Influence

Michael Novak, the renowned American philosopher, wrote that "several different types of cultures favor capitalist success: Protestant, Confucian, Jewish, Northern European Catholic. All of these have in common a certain rigor and austerity, an almost Stoic sense of sobriety and responsibility, and a certain disdain for corruption. In such cultures capitalism grows speedily."[3] As Novak recognized, there is a religious or spiritual foundation to the morality supporting successful capitalism—or by extension, successful businesses. As he declared unequivocally, "The only long-lasting foundation for a capitalist society is a moral, spiritual, and religious one."[4]

What does this have to do with Miele's success? Well, we know that Miele (and other successful *Mittelstand* companies) are *prudent* (the first P of common-sense business). They also demonstrate enormous *patience* and *practicality*. But they are also clearly *principled*. And these principles must come from somewhere. One obvious clue is that Miele's founders, Miele and Zinkann, were devout Protestants from a deeply religious part of Germany. While it is impossible to trace fully how the religious beliefs of the founders and early workers have shaped Miele's particular culture, there are at least three avenues.

The first relates to what Max Weber has pointed out in his seminal essay, *The Protestant Ethic and the Spirit of Capitalism*. Martin Luther, the father of Protestantism, introduced the idea of the "calling," the notion that "the fulfillment of worldly duties is under all circumstances the only way to live acceptably to God. It and it alone is the will of God, and hence every legitimate calling has exactly the same worth in the sight of God."[5] This idea gives powerful religious legitimation to the conduct of business. It's not only the priest, nun, or preacher who has a religious "calling" to fulfill. It's everyone in all walks of life. Such a spiritual understanding encourages a deeply serious and conscientious attitude toward work. With this philosophy, work *is* spiritual. Miele's founders and early workers had precisely this work ethic—that fact is easily observed—and they then successfully entrenched it in the firm.

The second influence on Miele's founders was the biblical notion of thrift. Thrift is a virtue that implies an attitude of spending wisely. And the underlying motive is not greed but gratitude: gratitude to God for the gifts He has bestowed, which leads spiritually inclined people to care for the gifts by not wasting them. Miele's founders and early workers were strongly influenced by this notion of thrift, and it has in turn translated into Miele's focus on responsible environmental stewardship and sustainable products.

The third religious influence on Miele is the Christian idea (both Protestant and Catholic) that a human being is created in the image of the Creator, and is called on to "be a co-creator and given the vocation to act creatively. Every co-creator is free, that is, expected both to assume responsibility and to show initiative."[6] This idea has proven very compatible with successful capitalism, which, as Novak wrote, "lies in discovery, innovation, and invention....Thus have new technologies been born and entire new industries (automobiles, airplanes, moving pictures, electronics, computers) been created."[7] The deeply innovative ethos of Miele, which has certainly generated many new products, dates back to the founders and continues to this very day. This too has at least some connection to the Christian notion that humanity has a vocation, a calling to be creative and solve problems.

Branding, Positioning, and Growth[8]

Miele's simple aim is to be "the most desirable brand in the industry in all relevant markets." Miele seeks to be a brand that has earned the deep trust and respect of consumers everywhere. To a large extent, Miele has achieved this goal. For example, in the "Best Brands" award initiated by GFK, a respected market-research organization, Miele is continually one of the top ten "Best Product Brands" and "Best Corporate Brands" from 2007–2014. Miele's success extends beyond Germany, and it has won consumer awards the world over. For example, in January 2011, *Which?* magazine awarded the "Most Reliable Domestic Appliance Brand" to Miele. In five product categories (Washing Machines, Tumble Dryers, Dishwashers, Freezers and Cylinder Vacuum Cleaners), Miele was also given the "Best Brand Overall." In the same year, the Australian Consumer Magazine *Choice* presented the "Choice" Award for "Best Washing Machine Brand" to Miele. Over time, Miele has built trust while raising expectations. To honor this trust and do justice to these demands is a great challenge—and a crucial success factor.

One of the ways the company has sustained such stellar reputation is through its rigorous strategic positioning. Instead of dividing its energies, Miele concentrates on building the value of a single brand by manufacturing quality. Miele basically bets that customers are willing to pay premium prices for premium quality. Thus, it has managed to remain profitable even though it has bucked the globalizing trend to outsource production to countries with lower labor costs. As Dr. Reinhard Zinkann explained, this decision is inseparable from Miele's values of innovation and quality:

> There is always going to be a market for the best, even if it's a bit more expensive. We try to think ahead. We want to set trends, not follow them. Our growth is based on our position as a leader in the field of technology and our ability to innovate. This is our interpretation of quality.[9]

In terms of growth, its strategy is underlined by tough financial prudence. It believes in financing its growth organically through family resources and reinvested profits, without major bank loans or recourse to the stock market or other external means. The company's management believes that such a strategy is very advantageous, allowing it to "think in terms of generations" and without the pressure for quarterly returns. Miele does not merely want to exploit a market for short-term gains, but "own that market, invest in it, and be engaged on a long-term basis." Additionally, a conservative and cautious spirit tempers growth at Miele. Dr. Zinkann explained:

> And a business does not usually collapse because of the bad times, but because of mistakes that were made during the good times; that means not feeling too comfortable when things are going well, but instead using that time to prepare for when things are not going quite so well. You have to ask yourself questions, even if it makes you feel uncomfortable. I think we managed to do that very early on.[10]

It is therefore unsurprising that Miele rarely engages in acquisitions to achieve leaps of greater revenue or market share. Instead, Miele prefers to grow organically by carefully penetrating a variety of international markets, releasing innovative new products and then building on those products (like becoming experts on home washing machines and then branching out into commercial washing machines). In this, they have been most successful. Over a century, the international growth of Miele has been steady, and Miele products are now found in almost a hundred countries. Miele has also invested steadily in research and development. The number of innovative products in Miele history is a true testimony to the success of their R&D process.

Recruitment[11]

To achieve growth and continue its tradition of producing the best products in the world, Miele needs to attract the most talented and dedicated employees. Dr. Markus Miele asserted that Miele's "quality demands cannot be fulfilled in glossy brochures. They must be reinforced every day and by every employee, whether a trainee or a manager; everyone must take responsibility." Thus, Miele places great emphasis on attracting talent. For instance, the company has many initiatives promoting Miele as a great employer for young people, and these initiatives target future employees before they even start an apprenticeship or enter university. One example is "Girls' Day" to attract schoolgirls to consider a Miele career. Another example is the OWL Maschinenbau network for innovation, a pilot project to help promote equal opportunities for German girls. This project aims to get schoolgirls excited about careers involving the technical subjects of math, information, natural science, and technology (MINT). It also helps to increase the number of female technical recruits for Miele.

Miele also offers grants to young students, particularly engineering students, consisting of both financial aid and an opportunity to gain actual work experience. Annually, Miele also welcomes visitors to the Gütersloh, Bielefeld, and Oelde plants to learn more about apprenticeships. In Gütersloh alone, a good 1,000 visitors (schoolchildren, teachers, parents) took this opportunity in 2013 to find out more about a Miele apprenticeship. Miele has also increased its presence at career fairs.

Miele's recruitment policy helps disadvantaged young people through one-year placement to develop their abilities. Since 2009, numerous people have improved their capability to enroll in apprenticeships in this way. Other activities include career days for eight-graders, special internships for students and teachers, and offers of intensive work placements.

Apprenticeships

Drawing on Germany's tradition of apprenticeship excellence, Miele offers apprentice training in thirty-five occupations. The quality of training is excellent, and Miele apprentices routinely obtain top marks in the exam by the Chamber of Industry and Commerce. In 2010/2011 and 2011/2012, twenty-six apprentices received this honor. In another testimony to the quality of training and rigor of selection, all apprentices who had finished their training in 2011/2012 were given offers to stay on at Miele.

From 1995, Miele has supported commercial and technical dual-training schemes, which combine school-based learning with work. Since 1995, Miele has supported 143 apprentices, giving them the possibility of launching successful careers.

Entry-Level Opportunities for Graduates

There are a number of entry-level opportunities for graduates. First, graduates can enter the Master@Miele program, which allows graduates with a bachelor's degree to pursue a master's degree while gaining actual work experience. The program for junior sales representatives, which was first implemented in 2011/2012, develops five graduates with talent for sales every year. Then there is the popular one-year training program mentioned above, which employs everyone who graduates successfully.

Miele recruits trainees of any nationality and offers overseas placement in one of Miele's subsidiaries or international plants, so that trainees can acquire the ability to deal with people of other cultures and races. Since 2007, Miele has also offered graduates the position of "technical assistant to the plant manager." Graduates taking up this job report directly to the plant manager and are prepared for future managerial roles. This program has already trained new manufacturing and development leaders with crucial technical roles in Miele.

Training and Development[12]

Once talented individuals are recruited, Miele is conscientious in training and developing them. The most important aspect of this is the dissemination of company culture. Primarily, this relies on the example set by company leaders, starting at the top with the executive directors. Next, for new staff, there are extensive inductions at which the corporate values are emphasized. Supporting all these are the stellar reputation of Miele and the prestige of a "Miele identity," which provide staff members both extrinsic and intrinsic motivations to live out Miele values.

Beyond this, Miele offers its employees training that is broad but targeted. It ensures that their workforce, whose average age is 46.1 years and counting, remains high performing. The company caters to this age group through programs offering flexible training options. It focuses increasingly on getting staff to acquire skills to collaborate internationally. Indeed, the number of international participants in talent-development programs is projected to increase to support the increasingly international nature of Miele's business. Finally, it seeks to internally raise its technical people and managers.

General Personnel Development

The general framework guiding Miele's human-resource development is its Excellence Model for Human Resource Development:

> The excellence model focuses on six core areas:
> *Learning management:* planning human-resource development through various forms of learning
> *Organizational management:* training and developing future managers

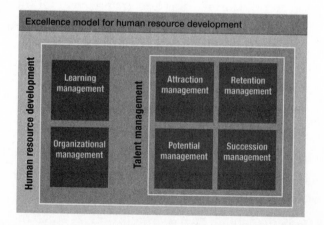

Attraction management: attracting new talented workers to Miele

Potential management: finding and training talent in the company early and well

Retention management: retaining employees through various means

Succession management: transparent and consistent succession planning

Miele invested approximately €16.4 million in personnel development in the financial year 2010/2011. Each employee trained for an average of 8.4 hours. Miele uses an electronic Learning Management System (LMS) to plan, execute, and monitor human-resource development. This also serves as an information-sharing platform and an e-learning tool.

In general, Miele's personnel development tracks the following process, circling from appraisal interviews to evaluation of benefits:

Targeted Personnel Development

Miele targets the development of its managers, following the principle of demanding and rewarding excellence. In line with this, the company strives to grow and promote managers from within.

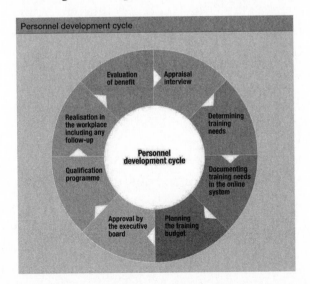

Miele uses a combination of live and online training for managers to help them master leadership and management. Experienced managers also mentor new employees, providing career-related advice, furnishing contacts, supporting project work, and giving feedback. Training sessions and personal coaching are also highly organized. The topics discussed range from leadership and time management to communication skills across cultures.

Targeted training also takes place for other segments of Miele's staff. For example, Miele customer service technicians have taken part in a national qualification course called "Successful Selling in Service." A new training program for developing experts in refrigeration/heat-pump technology was developed in 2011/2012: WissensWert ("worth knowing"). Over twelve days, external technical experts organized thirty-one workshops for eighty participants from different Miele plants. These participants could select the most useful and suitable modules for themselves, attending between three and eighteen modules each to gain their qualifications.

Networking and Knowledge Transfer

Miele also organizes an annual international "competitiveness symposium" at Gütersloh to allow officers of different ranks to exchange information. The participants are technical officers from German and international Miele plants, and they exchange and evaluate best practices and innovation, and discuss how these practices and innovation can be applied at other company sites.

Sustainability[13]

Miele products are developed and constructed to possess many features that make them friendly to the environment: long-term endurance, energy efficiency, "smart" features, and so on. "Quality" to Miele does not only mean building the best product for serving human needs but also the best product for efficiently consuming energy and conserving precious natural resources like water.

Legendary Durability

We've already lauded the durability of Miele products and how they test products with the view of at least twenty years' use in mind. To accomplish this durability, production and quality control processes are rigorous, and components and materials are carefully chosen. Even at the beginning, Miele's products—their early cream separators and butter churns—differentiated themselves from the competition because they were made from superior materials. Such qualities are well received by environmentally conscious customers. Products that last simply equal less waste.

For commercial appliances that can have high price tags, other companies tend *not* to put a high priority on conserving energy and resources, assuming that consumers will prefer the cheaper but less efficient machines. Thus, Miele provides detailed amortization calculations for the *entire* product life cycle, educating consumers to take into account their long-term performance needs as well as their energy costs.

Excellent Energy Efficiency

Miele, in its effort to perfect all possible facets of an appliance, focuses intensely on first-rate energy efficiency. Since 2000, the company has

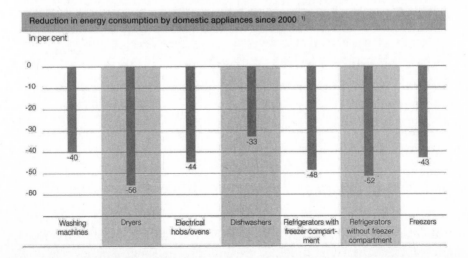

Reduction in energy consumption by domestic appliances since 2000 [1)]

drastically improved the efficiency of its products while not affecting (or even enhancing) their performance. All Miele appliances *are* the most energy efficient in their respective markets.

In 2011, Miele became the first European manufacturer to sell washing machines with the best energy efficiency rating: A+++. By 2011/2012, 54 percent of all their washing machines had attained this rating. A new type of heat-pump dryer was also introduced in 2011, which reduced energy consumption by approximately 20 percent compared to previous models and used less than half the energy consumed by normal condenser dryers. In addition, even their mid-price-range dishwashers now increasingly have the best energy efficiency rating, A+++.

Miele appliances have very low standby electricity consumption. (This matters, because only 80–90 percent of the total energy consumed by appliances in general is during actual usage.) Indeed, for many Miele appliances, this consumption has been cut to less than 0.1 watt—significantly better than statutory demands.

For commercial appliances, Miele has been working hard as well. In April 2012, a new type of commercial dishwasher was introduced: the ProfiLine range. Compared to the previous model, Miele has cut energy and water consumption by 10 percent while *enhancing* performance. The appliance received an excellent A+ efficiency rating—greatly improved from the C rating for the previous model. A new commercial dryer technology cuts energy costs by an astonishing 96 percent through using hot water from various sources, such as water warmed by solar and geothermal energy. Since December 2012, commercial washing machines (called "Little Giants") with an A+++ rated eco-cycle have been introduced.

In the political arena, Miele supports proposals for new and more stringent environmental requirements for new products. The company aim is to encourage legislation in this direction.

Eco-Friendly Functions

Miele augments its industry-leading energy efficiency with functions that the consumers can use to further optimize their energy and water consumption.

The Eco-feedback function, first introduced in 2009, which displays water and energy utilization, has helped consumers to cut energy efficiency significantly. Miele AllWater washing machines also help consumers to cut costs, as they can be used with hot *or* service water. Miele appliances also help to save detergents and minimize their harmful impact. Miele was the first manufacturer to build machines that automatically release detergent. On average, AutoDos has cut by 30 percent the amount of detergent used.

Finally, Miele not only provides the technologies for eco-friendly usage, it seeks to challenge consumers to change their habits and save costs. It does this by the provision of information through publications, face-to-face conversations, and various websites.

Low Emissions

As part of its focus on quality, Miele appliances must be made as perfect as possible in every way. Thus noise, odor, and moisture emissions are reduced to as low a level as possible. Dishwashers work with little noise and can be used in off-peak periods at night. Cooking devices like steam cookers or wall ovens have filters to minimize vapors and smells permeating the kitchen. The condensate leakage of Miele dryers is industry leading. Such low emissions improve product safety (enhancing the users' health) and enhance energy efficiency.

Gentle Processes

Customers who invest in Miele appliances also want their clothes and dishes to last—not just the machines that clean them. So Miele builds their appliances to wash gently. Again, this saves resources by prolonging the life of the items that are being cleaned. This is very important in places where significant quantities of dirty laundry or dishes are present, such as in nursing homes, caterers, or hotels.

Energy Intelligence

Miele was the first manufacturer in the world to build appliances that are Smart Grid ready. Appliances with the "SG Ready" label, like washing machines, tumble dryers, and dishwashers can function automatically when cheaper rates are available or when the solar power source at home provides sufficient electricity. In the early 2000s, Miele@home was launched to permit Miele domestic appliances to be connected *to* each other via power lines. Connected domestic appliances can now exchange information with a "Miele gateway," a compact box, also connected to existing power lines. The gateway can download information from energy companies and can then start appliances *automatically* at optimal times to reduce electricity costs. In this way, Miele has again been a pioneer in the arena of intelligent energy management.

Recyclability, Return, and Disposal

Miele's products are largely made up of metal (up to 90 percent) to aid in recycling. And in twenty-nine European Union countries, Miele has its own return and recycling systems (or they build upon existing national systems). Miele also actively participates in the continuous enhancement of recycling processes with waste management and recycling partners. Miele works through different associates and committees to encourage the establishment of high standards for waste management.

Future Efforts

Miele's goal is to increase by 20 percent the proportion of dishwashers, refrigerators, and washing machine with the top two energy-efficiency ratings (A++ and A+++) for the European market. Miele will also expand its range to include solar dryers and dishwashers augmented by solar panels. Eco-friendly features like SG Ready, Eco Feedback, and

AutoDos will also be further enhanced. Miele plans to invest in energy-recovery systems and optimized process technology to further reduce the water and energy usage of their commercial dishwashers.

Customer Service[14]

In October 2013, Miele won the Domestic and General Total Excellence & Quality (TEQ) Award in the Domestic Appliance Manufacturer Category for the seventh time (it has only been given out for sixteen years). The award recognizes manufacturers that have provided customers with great customer experiences during repair services over the past twelve months. The judging is based on 400,000 customer surveys, and 94.6 percent of those surveyed viewed Miele's customer service as being "good" or "excellent."

Indeed, excellent customer service is very much aligned to the company's core traditions. Dr. Markus Miele emphasized that "customer service after delivery of the product is also an important part of our quality assurance." They mean it. They won't even expand into a new country unless they can set up a functioning customer-service center there as well. It's the opposite of outsourcing!

In that vein, all Miele service technicians are also employed by Miele directly and trained in Miele's own academy. They receive regular training to ensure they are kept up to date. Even "authorized Miele service dealers" are trained in Miele's academy and need to deliver the same quality of service. To minimize the need for return visits and to speed up repairs, Miele technicians carry 90 percent of parts with them in their vans to every service call.

Environmental Stewardship in the Company Itself[15]

Besides manufacturing sustainable products, Miele continually improves its own energy efficiency in production processes and company buildings. For example, from 2009/2010 to 2011/2012, Miele managed to cut their own energy consumption by 8 percent. Since

2000, even while the company has grown, energy consumption has been reduced by 15 percent. Very efficient cooling units are used in Gütersloh to cool the computer center and to supply air conditioning. Once this initiative reaches its final stage, this will result in 2,000-megawatt hours of energy saved—enough to heat one hundred houses. In the medium term, Miele will also gradually transform administrative buildings and production facilities in Gütersloh to further cut the energy needed for heating.

Since May 2011, Miele has been involved in a learning network with thirteen other companies, aiming to reduce the use of 11,000 metric tons of CO_2 a year and decrease energy costs by €2.2 million a year. The companies hold weekly meetings and technical workshops to exchange experiences and strategies. Miele has also achieved success in reducing its carbon footprint. In 2010/2011, the company's carbon footprint was 95,850 tons; in 2011/2012, it was reduced by 0.9 percent, to 95,008 tons. More strikingly, CO_2 emissions per ton of product were reduced by 3 percent. This might not seem like a lot, but consider that it adds up every year: Miele has cut CO_2 emissions from energy consumption by 61 percent since 2000.

Miele's subsidiaries are also actively engaged in environmental protection. For example, the Norwegian subsidiary utilizes geothermal energy for heating and cooling; the Austrian and British subsidiaries plan to harness solar power for use; and the US offices are powered by renewable energy and have launched a variety of other environmental initiatives.

Miele seeks to educate and inspire employees to change their own behavior. They hold informational workshops about various ways to conserve electricity and other resources. They also provide guidelines at all offices on ways to reduce the use of paper, water, and electricity, and to increase recycling.

Community Involvement[16]

Miele seeks to help build a united and attractive community, wherever it operates. For example, in Germany, Miele invests in grants for the engineering disciplines. Beneficiaries include the Studienfonds Ostwestfalen (since 2007), RWTH Aachen University (since 2009), and Technische Universität Darmstadt (since 2011). Currently, Miele supports twenty-five students. In order to receive the grants, students demonstrate exceptional achievements and show evidence of community involvement. Miele also promotes culture and the arts in Germany. They sponsor the Gütersloh Boys' Choir and the renowned Westphalian Philharmonic Chamber Orchestra. Miele also assists in sports, integration, and disaster relief, including charitable donations.

In the United States, Miele supports various charitable organizations. The Japanese subsidiary promotes culture and sport. And the Spanish subsidiary invests in environmental protection.

Immer Besser? Competing in the Twenty-First Century[17]

Miele has clearly attained immense success in terms of building an international presence, revenues, and a prestigious brand. However, it faces a number of significant challenges as it seeks to expand internationally and keep its edge over competing companies in terms of quality and technology.

The first challenge is that Miele is already well entrenched in many affluent regions, such as Western Europe, the United States, and Japan. These are markets where premium appliances are demanded by a significant number of customers. However, the possibilities for significant future growth reside in fast-growing and populous countries such as India and China. Here, the obstacles to success can be both subtler and much greater. In India for instance, much of the population are far too poor to afford Miele products. In addition, while there are millions of Indians who are rich enough to afford luxury cars made by BMW, Audi, or Mercedes, one cannot simply assume that these same people will buy a luxury washing machine. The Head of Miele India, Dhananjay Chaturvedi, shared a story about one of the richest men in India. This tycoon owned multiple luxury cars, jets, and helicopters, and he indulged himself with the most expensive suits and watches. Yet he refused to spend on expensive home appliances. He asked, "Why should I spend Rs 3 lakh on a washing machine?" According to Chaturvedi, one reason for this is that rich Indians tend to engage in conspicuous consumption, flaunting highly visible and expensive goods. Many potential customers simply do not think it is sensible to buy an expensive product that will disappear into their kitchens. The idea of "quality" as defined by Miele just does not translate into something valuable in the minds of many rich Indians. Instead, most of Miele's customers are those who have travelled or lived overseas and "understand the subtlety of owning a premium home appliance."

Given such cultural obstacles, there are few existing distribution networks for expensive appliances. Miele India has found success by partnering with residential projects, fitting them with appliances. It also sells to institutions like hospitals and attempts to sell whole modular kitchens to affluent consumers. In general, while Miele has been very successful, it remains to be seen whether it possesses the ability to make its premium products competitive in developing markets with vastly different cultural and social dynamics from Western Europe. The question is whether new Chinese, Brazilian, and Indian consumers of the twenty-first century will find it worthwhile to pay premium prices for Miele quality.

Next, the quality and advanced features of appliances are now increasingly dependent on sophisticated computer and internet technologies. In 2013, for example, Samsung introduced a refrigerator with touchscreen control, powered by Google's Android operating system and integrated with a Samsung phone app. LG has launched a system that allows customers to text their robotic vacuum to send it scurrying around the home. Miele has of course been a pioneer of electronic controls and networked appliances, even introducing the first iPhone-controlled washing machine. However, its competitive advantage in engineering does not necessarily translate into commensurate strengths in software and internet services, especially when they are up against technology titans like Samsung or niche firms with specialized competencies like iRobot (a firm founded by MIT robotics scientists). For now, Miele does not believe in aping the competition but in taking a different, though perhaps more conservative, approach. As Dr. Miele explained:

> Ultimately, you have to look at what's really the consumer benefit. When you look at the connected appliance, does it really make sense to start it from your office when you still have to manually load and unload it? Interconnected appliances offer a broader range of benefits. We have a function called "smart start"—for instance, when you load a washing machine after lunch and you want to, it is ready by 7:00 a.m. tomorrow. The machine looks for the cheapest energy from your energy company and does it at 3:00 a.m. The intelligent usage of energy is interesting; interconnected doesn't necessarily just mean you can start from somewhere else.[18]

It remains to be seen whether Miele can continue to produce products, either on its own or in partnership, that are just as innovative and useful as those produced by their rivals who can tap into significantly greater strengths in computer technologies and networking.

On top of this, the increased importance of computer technology in home appliances poses a possible threat to one of Miele's core strategies: differentiating its products through their legendary durability. Computers, and related products like smartphones, advance notoriously fast, and few if any consumers hang on to their computers or smartphones for decades—the traditional Miele timeframe. If the advent of the "smart" home causes consumers to view app-controlled washing machines or robotic vacuum cleaners as being less like durable fixtures and more like transient desktop computers, then will Miele's tremendous investment in forging durable products be worthwhile? Indeed, will durability continue to be a mark of a truly better product?

For a hundred years, Miele has been an outstanding company that has maintained a fanatical focus on its core values of quality, innovation, and responsibility. It has endured through wars, economic miracles, and international expansion. It remains to be seen whether and how it can adapt to the exigencies of the twenty-first century while keeping true to its virtuous purpose and defining values. As technology advances rapidly and Miele approaches the limits of growth in developed markets, it will have a chance to prove to the world that it is truly "built to last."

NOTES

1. Some information in this section gathered from Tina Gant, ed., *International Directory of Company Histories* (St. James, 2004), vol. 56; "Miele & Cie. KG History," company profile, FundingUniverse (www.fundinguniverse.com); "The Miele Company: Journey Through Time," Miele & Cie. KG (miele.com), accessed October 22, 2014; and "Business Report 2013/14: Facts and Figures," Miele & Cie. KG (press.miele.com), accessed October 22, 2014.

2. Some information in this section gathered from "Sustainability Report 2013," Miele & Cie. KG (www.miele-sustainability.com), accessed October 22, 2014; "Better Living Begins with Miele," Miele & Cie. KG (www.mielepressroom.com), accessed October 26, 2014; "A Hands-on Company," Miele & Cie. KG (www.miele-project-business.com), accessed October 24, 2014; "More than 1 Million Items of Crockery Washed," Miele & Cie. KG (press.miele.com), accessed October 22, 2014; "Facts and Figures," Miele & Cie. KG (press.miele.com), accessed October 22, 2014; "A Hands-on Company," Miele & Cie. KG (www.miele-project-business.com), accessed October 24, 2014; "The Miele Company: Quality," Miele & Cie. KG (www.miele.com), accessed October 25, 2014; and Koeberle-Schmid, A., Kenyon-Rouvinez, D., and Poza, E., *Governance in Family Enterprises: Maximising Economic and Emotional Success* (Macmillan, 2014).

3. Michael Novak, "The Catholic Ethic and the Spirit of Capitalism," Stetson University (stetson.edu), accessed October 26, 2014.

4. Ibid.

5. Max Weber, *The Protestant Ethic and the Spirit of Capitalism*, trans. Talcott Parsons (New York: Routledge Classics, 2001), 84.

6. Novak, "Catholic Ethic and Spirit of Capitalism."

7. Ibid.

8. Some information this section gathered from "Sustainability Report 2013"; "Archives," Growth from Knowledge (bestbrands.de), accessed October 26, 2014; "International Awards," Miele & Cie. KG (www.miele-project-business.com), accessed October 25, 2014; and "A Hands-on Company."

9. "A Hands-on Company."

10. Ibid.

11. Some information in this section gathered from "Sustainability Report 2013: The Employees: Training and Education," Miele & Cie. KG (www.miele-sustainability.com), accessed October 24, 2014; and "A Hands-on Company."

12. Some information in this section gathered from "Sustainability Report 2013: The Employees: Training and Education."

13. Some information in this section gathered from "Sustainability Report 2013: Products and Supply Chain: Sustainable Products," Miele & Cie. KG (www.miele-sustainability.com), accessed October 22, 2014.

14. Some information in this section gathered from "Miele Wins Domestic & General Total Excellence & Quality (TEQ) Award," Domestic and General (corporate.domgen.com), accessed October 25, 2014; "A Hands-on Company"; and "Service and Repair," Miele & Cie. KG (www.miele.co.uk/support/serviceandrepair), accessed October 25, 2014.

15. Some information in this section gathered from "Sustainability Report 2013: Environmental Protection at the Company's Locations: Energy and Emissions," Miele & Cie. KG (www.miele-sustainability.com), accessed October 22, 2014.

16. Some information in this section gathered from "Sustainability Report 2013: Social Responsibility," Miele & Cie. KG (www.miele-sustainability.com), accessed October 22, 2014.

17. Some information in this section gathered from "Miele India's Head on

the Art of Selling High-end Goods," IBN Live (July 25, 2012) and Matt Warman, "Miele Prepares for Battle over the Machines of Tomorrow," *Daily Telegraph* (www.telegraph.co.uk) (February 16, 2014).

18. Matt Warman, "Miele Prepares for Battle."

PART III:
APPLYING COMMON SENSE

CHAPTER 12

TOOLS

Better to shun the bait than struggle in the snare.

—William Blake

An Oath of Virtuous, Common-Sense Capitalism

Our purpose is to serve the common good by bringing persons, all forms of capital, and communities together to create value that cannot be created alone. We emphasize stewardship for sustainable future economic growth and development. Using the virtues and the principle of subsidiarity, we seek the conditions for the articulation of new responsible leadership models and practices, centered on individual responsibility, care, and courage, with the capacity to better direct markets and wealth creation toward serving the person, cultural development, and human flourishing. We seek a course that enhances the value that enterprise everywhere around the globe can create for society, measured over the long term.

Therefore we promise:

- I will act with integrity and pursue work in an ethical and prudent manner.
- I will safeguard the interests of my shareholders, co-workers, and customers as well as the societies in which we operate.
- I will manage enterprise in good faith, guarding against decisions and behavior that advance narrow ambitions but harm the enterprise, the economy, and the societies it serves.

- I will understand and uphold, both in letter and in spirit, the laws and contracts governing my own conduct and that of the enterprise.
- I will take responsibility for my actions, and I will represent and recount the performance and risks of my enterprise accurately, with transparency and honestly.
- I will develop both myself and others under my supervision, so that the economy develops in a sustainable fashion and contributes to the well-being of the common good.
- I will strive to create virtuous economic, social, and environmental prosperity worldwide.
- I will be accountable to my peers, and they will be accountable to me, for living by this oath.
- This oath I make freely, and upon my honor.

Enterprise-Wide Risk Management: A Protocol[1]

Enterprise-wide risk management (ERM) programs and planning can play a critical role in improving business operations and mitigating risk and liability. They embody common-sense decision making as they identify, assess, and mitigate a wide number of risks. They are needed, because companies must think and plan about what to do in a crisis *before* they occur. Remember that the best steps to reduce exposure are prevention first; preparation second. ERM programs cover both bases.

ERM has become a global issue of applicability in large multinational companies doing business not only in the United States but elsewhere, around the globe. Think of BP's experience when in doubt! ERM involves best practices and recommendations that are relevant globally. Think News Corp! When done properly, ERM mitigates risks and reduces a company's litigation exposure. In extreme cases, it can prove to be critical to survival. It also can improve business operations by forcing more prudent behavior and a risk-adjusted analysis of profitability.

If you're not yet convinced that you need an ERM plan, consider that since the 2008 financial crisis, boards of directors and executive management are more than ever focused on new corporate-governance structures to develop an appropriate delegation of authority. There is a constant updating of risk management as well as the recruitment, selection, and orientation of all directors. Board charters, committee agendas, the running of board meetings, and determining who has authority to approve actions are all being reconsidered. Why? Because as we have seen, in crisis situations, every day brings yet more unimaginable events with catastrophic impact on employees, departures of key personnel, and hostile public and political environments. The velocity and unpredictability of such change and shocks cannot be anticipated. Therefore an effective ERM Plan is imperative for prudent business and rational action.

What kind of consequences flow from a serious incident? The politicization of the event, criminalization of corporate deeds, activist reaction by shareholders and the public. The sheer velocity of the consequences will make it impossible to cope without a plan already in place. Picture SEC, DOI, and FBI investigations, civil class actions, congressional hearings, internal investigations, and public/media scrutiny. Shareholders may try to split the CEO and chairman. Officer dismissals, significant market cap losses, ratings downgrades, and external investigations lie on the horizon. The unintended consequences mount fast, and publicity can be "sticky," seeming to last indefinitely.

Risk to consider vary by industry but include volatile financial environments, short selling, stock price pressure, chief executive conduct, succession, environmental and product liability, data security, breaches, export controls, and market disruption. Whistleblowers are on the rise as are cyber attacks, industrial espionage, labor events, strikes, stoppages, government actions, third-party business scandals, shareholder activism, and cloud computing failures.

You see why we emphasize that the only way to deal with such a crisis is to have a *plan* and a *team* in place *before* anything happens.

An ERM is the answer: it's simply a process and plan for identifying, assessing, managing, and mitigating risk. It is the first step for crisis management, litigation prevention, and loss mitigation.

What ERM Encompasses

All the risks a company faces, including financial market disruption, credit, interest rates, capital, human resources, transactional, data privacy, and legal need to be accounted. To be effective, your RM needs to be an *E*RM (across the entire enterprise). An ERM also considers enforcement actions by criminal authorities, governmental investigations, regulatory compliance, cyber attacks, technology threats, cloud computing, business continuity, operational risk, supply-chain risks, financial disclosure, document retention and disclosure, executive

misconduct, brand reputation, vendor relationships, business partners, third-party service providers, customers, and health and environment issues.

Who Requires an ERM Program?

Sarbanes-Oxley disclosure requirements demand an ERM, but the
federal and other sentencing guidelines and exchange governance
guidelines also require and reinforce them. Credit rating agencies
have incorporated ERM in their standards, and D&O liability and
litigation are now based on procedures in place. Accounting and audit
review standards for Internal Controls Certification require satisfac-
tory ERM, as do certain provisions of recent Dodd-Frank legislation.
These are more explicit for financial institutions, which require both
a separate risk-management committee at board level and a chief risk
officer with specific duties, powers, and reporting responsibilities.
Increasingly, new rules apply, calling for a focus from the board on
risk oversight, for risk-compensation policies, and for clear reporting
structures of key individuals who oversee total risk management.

Why ERM is Part of Common-Sense Business

ERM is essential to assess and analyze business activities on a risk-
adjusted basis. That way, prudent decisions can be made free from both
recklessness *and* paralyzing fear. This implies sound strategic planning
and financial management across every line of business. A higher rate of
return must be demanded from higher risk activities, as it will take
funds to pay for risk-mitigation efforts and all potential liabilities.

Common-sense business is always part of a proactive, preventative
compliance culture. It seeks to minimize and prevent risks. It mitigates
loss from failures. It prevents disasters, and it seeks to avoid litigation.

ERM must come from the top in any common-sense business; it
starts at the level of the board. This sends a clear message to officers,
employees, and the public at large that legal, ethical, and cultural

issues are imperative and that the firm represents sound, prudent business practices that are fused into the company's culture.

The board of directors must face all risks. The board must be apprised of the risks faced and be empowered to make independent determination that management has implemented and maintained effective ERM policies and procedures. This will include internal controls and compliance.

Assessment and Committee

An ERM identification and assessment should be undertaken by an independent third party. This assessment sets an appropriate risk-management process in place. Once completed, it should be implemented and updated routinely. The goal is to have a holistic approach to risk priorities, risk tolerance, and risk mitigation.

To prepare for the assessment, establish an ERM Committee. This committee should be composed of the CEO, senior executives from all lines and from IT, finance, audit, legal, compliance, human resources, public/investor relations, and geographical heads of business. It is essential to recognize the interdependency of products, geographies, and business lines and functions. This means empowerment—not a "tick the box" approach.

The ERM Committee assures that all risks faced by the company are identified, analyzed, and prioritized and that controls and procedures are in place to manage and mitigate those risks, with a focus on frequency and severity. The Committee should report directly to the Audit Committee of the board or a special Risk Committee, if in place. The chair of the ERM Committee should be considered the chief risk officer. The chair should hold updates and special meetings for the benefit of the board, to ensure information flow about key decisions, alternatives, and weighing of implications.

Risk must be assessed by the ERM Committee on an ongoing basis and include not just financial risk but every other facet of risk. Monthly meetings should be scheduled, recorded, and managed.

Formal presentations by each member of the ERM Committee should explain what processes and controls are in place to mitigate and manage risks. This is a "bottom-up" approach that utilizes information gathering, review, assessment, and mitigation recommendations. Recommendations on prioritization and tolerance need to be made as well. This is akin to a certification process, which means the company should take the process seriously. A decentralized approach is designed to more appropriately reflect, recognize, and assess risks at the operating levels.

A real crisis is like an iceberg; you can only see the smallest part sticking out of the water, but it's the mass underneath that can do the most damage. Because of this, a formal risk-prioritization scheme is mandatory. This should include stress testing and operational war games to determine risks and mitigation in extreme circumstances. Otherwise, you might find yourself handling the small part of the iceberg you can see and ignoring the dreadful crisis underneath.

Preparation is critical to get on top of a crisis, so your Committee must consider all kind of fallout, and they must be able to combine their solutions into an integrated, coordinated, holistic approach and response. (Of course, they don't have to come up with all this on their own. They will get the facts—all of the facts—from a quality independent investigation.) Realize that aside from legal consequences, crisis events generate customer, vendor, supplier, local, community, reputational, and employee reaction.

Since misinformation can create yet more problems, there must be a communications plan for information disclosure. Credibility must be maintained, and trust is important. No premature or false or misleading statements should be made. Your Committee may need to monitor social media to gather intelligence on what is happening and what messaging is occurring. Failure of boards to respond with a well-thought plan can result in creditors, suppliers, and customers acting irrationally, sending the company into a death spiral.

Moving forward, you ERM Committee should determine the frequency and scope of audits of each division. Audit results should be evaluated as a part of employee performance evaluations. Assessments should reflect a heat mapping of probability and severity, and the full board should see the results. The ERM Committee should also review all new products, geography expansions, and business initiatives. This will become a regular process of calculating risk-adjusted profitability.

When a crisis materializes, an ERM plan should be in place to minimize loss and mitigate litigation. It will have numerous elements, from public relations to the role of the board, to political, regulatory, enforcement, reputational, and legal strategies. These are simultaneous, not serial in nature. A wide-reaching ERM plan, if it has been properly developed, will assist in mitigating risk and would serve the company well should litigation or criminal enforcement ensue.

The Sustainability Audit™

A sustainability strategy, with performance management and auditing, along with comprehensive reporting on a continuous basis, has become imperative for responsible companies today no matter where you are headquartered or where you do business.

Since the late 1990s, the Global Reporting Initiative (GRI) has formulated and sought to implement a common framework for enterprise-level reporting on linked aspects of sustainability: environmental, economic, and social. This now encompasses the whole corporation, not just operations but also factors indirectly tied to the corporation. This balanced approach toward all performance of the enterprise looks at progress toward sustainable development. Auditability is crucial to scrutinizing reported information in order to discern credibility and accuracy and to hold companies accountable for their actions.

Such practice will satisfy requirements in corporate governance, business ethics, environmental concerns, health and safety management, social responsibility, strategy and economics, and responsible supply-chain management and reporting, while providing greater assurance for a company's nonfinancial data and information.

In the words of one leading expert,

Sustainable business development is a strategic management framework for leading change using enterprise thinking, visionary leadership, strategy and business integration, and innovation. It requires a holistic view of the business environment taking in social, economic, and environmental considerations as well as more conventional concerns of customers, markets and competition. It involves defining, assessing, and improving the whole business enterprise to achieve superior and sustainable performance that exceeds the challenges of the present and the expectations for the future.[2]

It is necessary to conduct regularly, then, Sustainability Audits, so as to satisfy legal requirements and to identify and mitigate all related risks. Sustainability Audits allow a company to check adherence to their Codes of Conduct. They should involve all strategically important suppliers and be conducted using a trusted third party (such as chartered consulting firms, the "Big Four" accounting firms, and firms like SGS that specialize in sustainability).

The benefits of a Sustainability Audit are many and include the following:

- Risk awareness
- Identification of strengths and weaknesses
- Continuous improvement
- Mitigation of risks
- Performance improvement
- Connections to customers and suppliers
- Legal compliance

As more and more states and governments impose rules and regulations in this area, it is important to review all the legal issues surrounding compliance in all the places you and your suppliers do business. Focus on the following:

- Prohibitions against corruption and bribery
- Reporting on human rights abuses
- Prohibitions against forced and child labor
- Health and safety issues and regulations
- Environmental protection
- Supply-chain compliance
- Energy efficiency and waste management

This is a rigorous step-by-step process that cannot be telescoped or short-sighted. It requires time, energy, and a budget and is best put in the competent hands of an external Sustainability Audit team.

The audit makes use of a consistent rating system an minor, major, and critical breaches, while identifying issu provement. It relies on a procedure-bound set of exerc process starts in a meeting of all concerned parties. It then factory and office inspections. It interviews employees and v takes the same processes to suppliers. It concludes by issuing and review. It often ends with a public meeting to discuss results and actions. The process comes up with what is called a "Corrective Action Plan." Companies need to execute on the violations cited and make continuous improvements over time.

Who Needs Sustainability Audits?

Have you heard the adage, "You only have to floss the teeth you want to keep?" Well, you only have to audit the businesses you want to keep, too. Companies of all sizes around the world today need independent assurance of their sustainability, and these programs add credibility to published information on corporate responsibility in addition to providing accurate and consistent reporting mechanisms. Sustainability Audits are also critically important in new investments or divesting parts of a business so as to determine the nature and extent of environmental, health and safety, and social liabilities. Many companies are also demanding carbon strategies to identify ways to reduce direct and indirect carbon emissions and to form approaches to carbon offsets and trading.

Sustainability Audits are becoming a normal part of the prudent business landscape. They allow a company to identify "best practices." They make sustainability planning and accounting more measureable and documentable. They also allow companies to launch new initiatives. They demonstrate tracking—period over period. And lastly, they lead to higher performance and long-term sustainability for those who engage them. They just make common sense.

If you're interested in learning more, the best single volume on the subject of sustainable business is David L. Rainey's *Sustainable*

Business Development: Inventing the Future through Strategy, Innovation, and Leadership (Cambridge University Press, 2006).

The Ethics Audit™

Do company leaders communicate regularly about the importance of ethics?

Do top leaders care about ethics and make them a priority?

Does avoidance of trouble with the law serve as an important reason why ethics matter at the company?

Are earning and keeping a good reputation based on ethics important at the company?

Is social responsibility a feature of ethics at the company?

Is being a good steward of the environment seen as important at the company?

Is maintaining strong financials and committed investors an important reason for ethics in the company?

Is maintaining good working relationships with business partners and vendors an important reason for ethics at the company?

Is customer acquisition and loyalty seen to depend on ethics at the company?

Are recruiting and retention of employees dependent on having an ethical organization?

Do the company's people take pride in the good ethics practiced there?

Does the company cut ethical corners?

Is ethics more than public relations at the company?

Is ethics part of the core identity of the company?

Is living by company values and ethics essential to the corporate mission?

Does the company stress the importance of being responsible as ethical citizens in the communities where it operates?

Would the company do the right thing even if it cost something?

Would the company do the right thing if it did not have a financial benefit?

Would the company do the right thing if competitors did not follow suit?

Is the company motivated to be ethical?

Are people in the company unethical?

Does the company violate laws and regulations?

Does the company violate company or professional standards?

Does company behavior bother you and your conscience?

Does the company violate the Golden Rule?

Does the company combat controversy, scandal, and public distrust?

Could someone be seriously harmed or irreparably damaged by the ethical behavior of the company?

Is the role of ethics spelled out in the company?

Can people speak to an objective third party for advice or concerns about ethics?

Can people approach their immediate supervisor or boss about ethics?

Does the company have channels such as hotlines, HR, or an ethics officer?

Can you blow the whistle at the company by going outside normal channels?

Does the company take ethics cases seriously?

Does the company work to clarify ethical issues and consult on them?

Does the company consider all of the consequences of ethical issues?

Does the company "buy time" in ethics cases and drag its feet?

Does the company strive to resolve ethics cases?

Does the company take follow-through actions in ethics cases?

Are ethics offenders dealt with properly and fairly?

Does the company reform its ethical culture regularly?

Is there sufficient ethics training at the company?

Does the company make constant attempts to change and improve its ethical culture?

Does the company have effective methods for troubleshooting in an ethical crisis?

Do all employees know how to recognize ethical problems when they arise?

Do all employees know what to do when they encounter an ethical question or violation?

Are people encouraged to ask questions about ethics?

Are people discouraged or punished for asking ethical questions?

Does the company have a safe, confidential process for people to report or discuss ethics violations or dilemmas?

Does the company act prudently and quickly to address ethical questions and problems?

Is the company open, honest, and transparent in its mistakes?

Does the company cover up its ethical lapses?

Does the company examine and reform structural factors that cause or permitted crisis?

Are ethical failures at the company treated as opportunities to learn?

Are ethical failures at the company seen as opportunities to punish those responsible?

Are ethical dilemmas handled well and resolved efficiently at the company?

Are ethics troubleshooting and response systems and procedures in place and working at the company?

Is the long-term ethical health of the company and effect on performance recognized?

Does the company work to build an ethically healthy organization?

Does the company strive to identify ethics issues?

Does the company educate around those ethics issues?

Does the company implement policies, practices, and procedures around ethical issues?

Does the company evaluate what it is doing on ethics?

Does the company consider ethical motivations as a rationale?

Does the company manage crises?

Does the company have a resolution method for ethical issues?

Does the company include ethics in its shared core mission/ vision?

Does the company embed ethics in its culture?

Does the company have robust, reliable, principle-guided practices?

Do company leaders sustain an ethical vision and systems?

Do top leaders play a significant role in ethical training?

Are people held accountable for ethical decisions?

Are there organizational ethics assessments?

Are ethics focus groups used at the company?

Does the company use internal/external ethics research?

Are personnel evaluations ethical?

Are ethical statements posted?

Is ethics training annual?

Is ethics training online?

Is ethics training done in live classes?

Does the company tell stories about the ethics of its founders and continuing mission?

Are key pieces of company literature focused on ethics?

Is the company admired for its ethics?

Can the company be described as an ethical company in its products and services?

Is the company better at ethics than its competitors?

Is the company at the top of ethical standards in its industry?

Does the company always treat customers ethically?

Do others describe the company as ethical, such as competitors, journalists, and customers?

Does the company have a clear, strong, inspiring core mission and vision that is ethical?

Are the mission and vision statements inspirational and ethical?

Does everyone at the company know and understand that mission and vision?

Does the mission and vision guide all business decisions?

Does the company "walk the talk"?

Do the leaders of the company focus the organization on pursuing an ethical purpose?

Do the managers focus on the same purpose?

Do employees have a regular ability to comment on the ethics, purpose, and mission of the company?

Does the company mission and vision align with your personal ethics?

Are the core defining characteristics or traits of the company embedded in all parts of the organization and every office?

Do these characteristics affect every person hired, every geographical location, and every project?

Does the company do a good job orienting and training around cultural values and ethics?

Does the company architecture—office set up and equipment—express core values and ethics?

Is the organizational chart and compensation system ethical?

Does the company strive to hire people who are ethical and the "right fit"?

Does company culture and management operate in an ethical manner?

Does the company always work within the law?

Does the company always treat workers right?

Does the company try to always do the right thing?

Does the company have systems to help people overcome ethical temptations or challenges in the workplace?

Are the company's guidelines clear to avoid getting into ethical trouble?

Are ethical principles articulated well in a code of ethics at the company?

Is the code of ethics enforced?

Does the company have clearly identified ethical principles that provide guidance for daily work?

Are ethical principles not just negative but positive behaviors to be pursued?

Does the company do well in training all new employees in ethics?

Do all levels of responsibility in the company understand the code of ethics?

Are ethical blind spots and updates part of the company ethics practices?

Is the statement of ethics made available to clients, business partners, vendors, government agencies and the public?

Are internal controls focused on ethics?

Is the leadership effective around ethics?

Do the leaders and managers perform ethically?

Do the leaders and managers remind employees of the core mission, vision, and ethics?

Is there a culture of integrity at the company?

Does the company mentor and train future leadership candidates on ethics?

Does the company track ethical failure?

Does ethics figure into leadership transitions?

Is the company more ethical than other places you have worked?

Does your company have a corporate social responsibility statement and report?

Does the company take seriously your own moral compass?

Does the company fit your own ethical management principles?

Is corporate governance ethical at the company?

Does the Board of Directors get ethics training?

Does the Board of Directors see ethical challenges in the company?

Does the Board of Directors evaluate the leadership based on ethical practice and achievements?

Does the Board of Directors adequately oversee an ethics audit?

Does the company adequately involve external counsel in its ethics programs?

Does the company adequately involve external ethics consultants in its programs?

Does the company adequately involve crisis management firms in its ethics programs?

Does the company adequately involve its D&O liability insurer in its ethics programs?

Does the company adequately involve its search firms in its ethics programs?

Is the company conscious of programs to lower operating costs based on ethics?

Is there an Enterprise Risk Management program in place at the company?

Does the company treat all people with respect as valuable individuals?

Does the company communicate ethics across all divisions with care and respect?

Does the company model and encourage a balanced ethical life?

Does the company honor and respect the families of all?

Does the company protect the life, safety, and health of all?

Does the company keep its commitments and agreements as trustworthy?

Does the company promote fairness in matters of money and property?

Does the company communicate truthfully and constructively?

Does the company cultivate a positive ethical attitude?

Is the company open to your suggestions on improving ethics?

The Corporate Governance Audit © ™ 3
Corporate Objectives

Does your company have an objective strategy and plan on sustainable shareholder value?

Does it include the management of governance?

Does it include nonmaterial aspects? All financial aspects?

Does your company have a strategy and plan covering stakeholders? Employees? Suppliers? Customers? The local communities where you operate? The environment?

Corporate Board Responsibilities

Do the members of your Board act as fiduciaries?

Are they accountable to the shareholder body?

Do they act in the best interest of the company?

Does your Board have effective debate around current operations? Potential risks? New developments?

Does the Board have independent leadership?

Does the Chair create and maintain a culture of openness?

Is a diversity of views expressed and encouraged?

Are various competencies and diversity of perspectives present on the Board?

Is the discussion on the Board challenged?

Is there independent direction of the executive team?

Does the nonexecutive element on the Board have enough information and knowledge of the business to contribute effectively?

Is enough information on performance provided and in a timely fashion?

Is the Board conscious of its accountability to shareholders for its actions?

Does the Board review, approve, and guide corporate strategy?

Does it discuss all major plans of action?

Does it understand corporate risk policy?

Are all business plans addressed?

Does it set performance objectives?

Does it monitor implementation and overall performance?

Does it assess the CEO? And the Board itself?

Does it oversee major capital expenditures? All acquisitions? All divestitures?

Does it oversee the integrity of accounting and reporting systems?

Is the audit independent?

Are controls in place?

Do they cover financial and operational control?

Do they cover compliance with the law and various standards and bodies?

Do they ensure a formal and transparent board nomination and election process?

Does it select, remunerate, monitor, and replace key executives?

Is there succession planning in place?

Is compensation aligned with long-term interests?

Does the Board have a formal risk management process?

Is this updated at least annually?

Does the Board monitor and manage potential conflicts of interest?

Does such a plan cover management? Board members? Shareholders? External advisors? And service providers?

Is there a specific characterization for misuse of corporate assets and related party transactions?

Is the Board monitoring the effectiveness of company governance practices?

Does it realign the company regularly with established best practices?

Is there an objective process of self-evaluation regarding behavior and effectiveness?

Does the Board oversee the process of disclosure and communications, especially to shareholders?

Can the Board call management independently to account?

Does the Board meet at times without management present?

Composition and Structure of the Board

Does the Board have a requisite skill range?

Does it have extensive competencies?

Does it have numerous strengths of knowledge and practice?

Is its experience rich and varied?

Does it have diversity?

How is that diversity measured?

Are numerous perspectives present at all meetings?

Does the Board discharge its duties and responsibilities effectively?

Do Board members allocate sufficient time to their duties?

Is leeway made when more time and effort is demanded?

Is full disclosure required of outside roles? Participation on other
     Boards? Are these limited?

Does the Board exercise independent judgment?

Is the Board free of external influencers?

Is it competent in key industry sector knowledge and experience?

Is there a majority of independent Directors?

Have those Directors had a number of years outside the com-
     pany before joining the Board?

How many Board members are former employees?

What is the length of tenure for Board members?

Are their interests aligned with those of executives? With share-
     holders?

Is independence practiced as a state of mind?

Does the company make adequate disclosures on its definition
     of independence?

Are deviations disclosed and explained?

Are members obliged to act as fiduciaries?

How do they exercise objective judgment?

Are there separate subcommittees for Audit? For Remuneration?
     For Governance? For Nomination?

Is there a separate and independent Risk Committee?

Are the remit, composition, and accountability and working pro-
     cedures of all Board subcommittees defined and disclosed?

Do committees report regularly and formally to the Board as a
     whole?

How are difficult issues handled?

Are the subcommittees and all nonexecutive audit and remuneration subcommittees solely independent?

The Chair

Does the Chair set the right context for the Board agenda?

Does the Chair make provision for the flow of information to Directors?

Does the Board allow and encourage open boardroom discussions?

Does the Chair enable debate?

Does the Chair provide, create, and maintain a culture of openness?

Does the Board allow a diversity of views to be expressed?

Is the Chair a former CEO?

Is the Chair independent on the date appointed?

Does the Chair participate in executive remuneration plans?

If the Chair is not independent, are there problems arising?

Is the structure under review?

Is the Chair available to shareholders for dialogue? Present at all meetings?

Is there a Lead Director?

Are all Board members available for shareholder meetings?

Does the Board appoint the Lead Director?

For what term?

Is that Lead Director fully independent?

Does the Lead Director lead the Board?

Does the Lead Director set the agenda?

Do they act as spokesperson for independent Directors?

Is the Lead Director able to raise critical issues?

Is he/she a conduit for shareholders to raise issues?

Does the Lead Director make him/herself available to fulfill this role?

Company Secretary

Does the company Secretary make all necessary information available?

Is this done on a timely basis?

Is the person a channel to seek independent expertise?

Does the Secretary provide access to needed expertise?

Do they provide practical guidance as to duties and responsibilities?

Is the Secretary informed on law and current regulation?

If the company does not have such a role have they considered appointing one?

Directors

Do Directors have appropriate knowledge?

Do they have access to operations and staff?

Do Directors make visits to the company?

Do they have insight into the company culture?

Company performance?

Organizational behaviors?

Do Board meetings allow time to challenge senior executives?

Are these matters considered at Board meetings?

What is the appointment?

Are mechanisms in place to ensure Director accountability to shareholders?

Is it done on an ongoing basis?

Do Directors stand for election annually?

Do Directors face evaluation frequently?

Do shareholders have a separate vote on the election of each Director?

Is information and time allotted for making a considered voting decision?

Is information on the appointment procedure disclosed at least annually?

Can shareholders nominate Directors by proposing candidates?

Can this be done to Committees?

Can it be done directly on the company's proxy?

Are the competencies and professional and related backgrounds of all Directors disclosed?

Are recent and current mandates disclosed?

Are best practices disclosed?

Is Board and committee attendance disclosed?

Are overall qualifications disclosed?

Are the shareholdings of Board members disclosed?

Is there a process of succession planning for non-executive members of the Board? For senior management?

Is a formal process of induction in place for all new Directors?

Is this done as early as possible?

Do Directors participate in training and education to assist them in their role more effectively?

Is regular evaluation of the Board and each of its Directors done routinely? Annually?

Are consultants engaged in this process?

Is evaluation of Board members done prior to renomination?

Are evaluations disclosed?

Are the lessons learned disclosed?

Are subcommittees equally evaluated?

Are all related party transactions reviewed and monitored?

Is a committee charged with reviewing significant transactions to determine what is fair?

Does the company disclose all such details in its annual report?

Is there a process for identifying and managing conflicts of interest?

If a Director has such an issue, is he/she allowed to participate in those discussions?

Are Directors informed on shareholder and public perceptions so as to avoid appearance of conflict of interest?

Corporate Culture

Is there a culture that ensures employees engage in appropriate behavior?

Does the Board encourage an ethical corporate culture?

Are active measures taken to ensure that ethical standards are adhered to across the business?

Does it extend to vendors, subcontractors, and supply chains?

Are yearly ethical audits performed?

Is there a Chief Ethics Officer?

Is regular ethics training conducted?

Does it encourage a culture of integrity?

Are the vision, mission, and objectives of the company ethically sound?

Codes of Conduct

Has a Code of Conduct been developed at the company?

Does it stipulate the ethical values as well as specific guidelines?

Does it cover both internal and external stakeholders?

Is the Code communicated across the company?

Is it integrated into company strategy and operations?

Are programs in place to promote the Code?

Does such training apply them effectively?

Are sufficient support and compliance assessments in place to gauge performance?

Are such Codes regularly considered for completeness and appropriateness?

Is the setting aside of any Codes discussed at Board level?

By shareholders?

Are stringent policies and procedures in place governing bribery and corruption?

Is the company complying with all guidance on anti-corruption practices and laws?

Does the company have clear rules on trading by Directors and employees in the company's own securities?

Does it make sure that individuals do not benefit from knowledge that is generally not available to the market?

Are all laws complied with in the jurisdictions where the company operates?

Does the Board have whistle-blowing provisions?

Are such mechanisms spelled out in detail?

Are fear of retribution concerns handled appropriately and confidentially?

Risk Management

Is the Board able to understand and insure that proper risk management is in place for all material and relevant risks?

Is the risk-management process dynamic and ongoing?

Does it identify all risks?

Does it measure potential outcomes and proactively manage to the extent appropriate?

Does the Board measure the company's total risk-bearing capacity? Limits for tolerance? Limits for key risks?

Does it avoid exceeding appropriate risk appetites?

Does the Board seek external counsel and support to supplement internal resources?

Is the risk plan approved at least annually?

Is the risk plan fully implemented?

Is risk identification broad and not just financial?

Are non-financial risks considered?

Is reputational risk considered?

Is all risk information disclosed?

Are management procedures for measuring and mitigating risk sufficient?

How is the robustness of such measures evaluated?

Are other than key risks disclosed?

Remuneration

Is remuneration for all key senior managers disclosed?

Are the time scales appropriate for the business and the shareholders?

Does executive pay incentivize the interests of executives with those of shareholders?

Do the structures and frameworks reinforce the corporate culture?

Are all considerations taken into account so as not to reward taking inappropriate behavior or risks at the expense of the company?

Is performance measured over timescales sufficient to determine that value has in fact been created?

Are guidelines for remuneration followed?

Is an outside study of comparable performance made?

Is pay for non-executive Directors structured?

Is it made payable so that risks compromising independent guidelines are followed?

Transparency

Does the company make disclosure of all significant aspects of its business, including remuneration and performance metrics?

Are risk-management considerations aligned between executives and shareholders?

Are all awards provided as well as the determination on how they were made disclosed?

Are all advisers to various committees disclosed and independent?

Is the ownership of shares of the company by senior managers and Directors provided annually?

Is use of derivatives or other structures to hedge share ownership or unvested equity-linked remuneration?

Are there company policies barring such hedging?

Is equity-linked remuneration subject to shareholder approval?

Are frameworks for aligning executive incentives in place?

Does the Board proactively seek dialogue with shareholders to address concerns on structures and frameworks aligned with corporate culture?

Are all risk considerations incorporated?

Are all rewards for inappropriate risks or behaviors disclosed?

Are the timescales used sufficient?

Do Boards of the promotion and enhancement make shareholders aware to corporate culture?

Audit

Does the company employ robust, independent, and efficient audit processes?

Does it use external auditors?

Does it have robust internal audit functions and controls?

Is the annual audit an objective opinion, and does it attest to fairly represent the financial statements and position of the company?

Does it cover all material aspects of the company?

Does it give a true and fair view of the affairs of the company?

Is there compliance with all applicable laws and regulations?

Has the Audit Committee agreed to the scope of the audit?

Do shareholders have the right to expand the scope of the audit?

Do the shareholders vet it?

Does the audit committee have regular dialogue with the external auditors?

Is management present? If an auditor, is it disclosed on a timely basis?

Are the auditors observing high-quality standards and ethical behavior?

Are all material vendors disclosed and approved in advance by the audit committee?

Are they disclosed in the annual report?

Is the audit firm rewarded in any way for selling other services?

Are internal audit functions in place?

Does that function have the respect, confidence, and cooperation of the Board and management?

If conflicts exist, does the Board disclose why in its annual report?

Does it explain how adequate assurance has been maintained in their absence?

Is there a reporting line to the audit committee chair?

Is the committee responsible for appointment?

For performance?

If outsourced, how is this function evaluated?

Does the external auditor provide internal audit services to the company?

Does the audit committee of the Board on behalf of the shareholders oversee the function?

Is independence and oversight of the quality of the audit sufficient?

Are all records documented and maintained?

Does the Board recommend removal of or reappointment of external auditors?

Is the process of independence of external auditors disclosed?

Disclosure

Does the company aspire to open and transparent communication?

Does this cover aims, challenges, and failures?

Is relevant disclosure and material information made available on a timely basis?

Is it provided to all shareholders and investors to make informed decisions?

Does it cover acquisitions? Ownership? Obligations? Rights? And the sale of shares?

Does the Board affirm with the company officers the company's financial statements and financial accounts?

Are such statements made available for all international investors in accounting and financial reporting standards, which are generally associated with high-quality international standards?

Are all accounting policies disclosed in the annual report?

Does the audit committee maintain oversight of key accounting judgments as an essential part of the disclosure to investors and shareholders?

Are guidelines followed for reporting all non-financial business reporting?

Is Corporate Social Responsibility reporting done? Environmental reporting?

Is information on results, company objectives, risk factors, stakeholder issues, and governance reported?

Is the company relationship to other companies in the corporate group and to major shareholders disclosed?

Shareholder Rights

Does the Board assure shareholders of accountability for board actions?

Have the corporate charter and articles of association been clearly set out?

Have all changes to such been subject to shareholder approval?

Has the Board done their utmost to enable shareholders to exercise their rights? To vote? To avoid hurdles?

Is divergence from one share–one vote always disclosed and justified?

Are there structures and protections in place for minority shareholders?

Do shareholders have the right to participate in key corporate governance decisions?

Can they nominate, appoint, or dismiss Directors? External
auditors?

Do shareholders control the nature of the company?

Have shareholder rights plans or poison pills been approved by
shareholders?

Are votes taken on any significant matters on a preemptive basis?

Do shareholders give permission for new issues of shares?

Can a specified portion of outstanding shareholders call a meeting of shareholders? How are such proposals handled?

Are provisions to a shareholders meeting permitted?

Are shareholders provided the right to ask questions of the
Board, management, and external auditors both before and
during meetings of shareholders?

Can they address matters concerning the Board, its governance,
its makeup, and the external audit?

Do institutional shareholders face regulatory barriers on voting
decisions or basic shareholder rights?

Is the exercise of ownership rights by all shareholders facilitated?

Is diligence of all matters proposed for shareholder vote provided?

Are votes by intermediaries cast in accordance with instructions
of the beneficial owner or authorized agent?

Can all votes or those made in absentia be properly counted and
recorded?

Are votes announced on a timely basis and published for each
resolution promptly after each meeting?

Are there rights of action and remedies that are readably accessible
to redress conduct of a company that treats them inequitably?

Are there minority shareholder protections and remedies against
abusive or oppressive conduct?

Does the company maintain a record of the registered owners of
its shares? Of those with voting rights over shares? Of registered owners of shares?

How is the company enabling shareholders to exercise these
rights?

Shareholder Responsibilities

Are shareholders encouraged to act so as to promote the company's objective of long-term value creation?

Are all shareholders, including pension funds, encouraged to be responsible for long-term value on behalf of their beneficiaries?

Are all shareholders encouraged to participate in a dialogue with companies to achieve common understanding of objectives?

Are pension fund shareholders insisting that their fund managers put sufficient resources into governance analysis?

Do shareholders take governance factors into account and consider the riskiness of a given business model?

Do shareholders have a role and way to contribute to the functioning of the Board? To the accountability of management? To the promotion and dissemination of information?

Do shareholders actively collaborate where this enables them to achieve effective results?

Do shareholders always vote on policies, practices, and priorities?

Do institutional shareholders subscribe to principles laid out in various international transparency and accountability bodies across the investment chain?

Do institutional shareholders conduct their own internal corporate governance and oversight of management?

NOTES

1. Robert Bostrom, former senior partner, Greenberg Trauig LLC, is acknowledged for some of this material and ideas shared in numerous conversations and presentations.

2. David L. Rainey, *Sustainable Business Development.* (Cambridge University Press, 2006).

3. The Corporate Governance Audit is based on the Green Paper of the European Union, The Principles of the Conference Board, and the ICGN Corporate Governance Principles (revised 2009), as well as definitive academic literature on the subject, such as Jonathan Macey, *Corporate Governance: Promises Kept, Promises Broken* (Princeton University Press, 2008).

CHAPTER 13
COMMON SENSE IN THE NOT-FOR-PROFIT SECTOR

The not-for-profit sector, which comprised 5.6 percent of the United States' GDP in the third quarter of 2016,[1] is composed of organizations commonly referred to as nonprofits. We don't like that these organizations are called by what they are *not*, but nonetheless they are vital to our economies and to civil society.

Nonprofits are built to achieve a specific mission that serves the public, and they do not earn profits for or pay dividends to any group or individual. Instead, nonprofits reinvest their revenue into the organization itself—its assets and its programs—to improve upon its mission. However, despite being designed to serve the public need, this sector is often blighted by instances of improper management, unethical practices, and perhaps most concerning, a lack of common sense. This lack is reflected in how the sector often becomes overly reliant on aid from others and how its organizations are improperly managed or lacking in transparency and accountability.

Because the not-for-profit sector receives substantial benefits, such as tax exemption on mission-related income, and because it is responsible for stewarding public and donor money, it must make changes to address its issues and behave more sensibly. Many solutions exist, but creating new revenue streams to lessen the reliance on public gifts, properly compensating employees, and improving internal controls while making commitments to transparency—these are among the most important ones.

New Revenue Streams

The not-for-profit sector should act more prudently by committing itself to creating new revenue streams in order to become less reliant on funding from sources like foundations or the government, which can fluctuate. In 2015, 21.3 percent of revenue in the not-for-profit sector came from private contributions and government grants (no services or goods provided).[2] That's over one-fifth of all funding. Many organizations have become overly dependent on this revenue and keenly feel any decreases. While certain sections of the not-for-profit sector, particularly colleges and universities, have dealt with decreases by raising the cost of tuition, other organizations have displayed prudence by creating alternate revenue streams to supplement their income and make them less dependent on funding sources that could disappear at any time.

Merchandise and gift stores can be a key revenue stream that many nonprofits don't have or utilize effectively. However, certain nonprofits have spent the time and care to develop their gift stores and their merchandise into a stable, significant business. Not only are the online and physical stores strategically positioned in areas with high foot traffic, but their selection of goods caters to a variety of interests. Although merchandising requires significant work and resources, it can prove well worth the effort for nonprofits.

Some nonprofits have created a revenue stream by renting out their facilities for events such as private parties, corporate meetings, and weddings.[3] Although this option isn't available to the entire not-for-profit sector, those organizations that own their own facilities should seek to maximize their options in this way.

Beyond allowing organizations to become less reliant on external funding sources, revenue generated from streams such as merchandise and facility rentals can be used for general overhead, which is an area for which nonprofits historically struggle to raise donations; donors prefer to designate their gifts for charitable programs. Although care needs to be taken to ensure that focus on these revenue streams doesn't deter an organization from its overall mission, it's common-sensical for the not-for-profit sector to diversify funding by developing new, internal sources of revenue. This will lead to more self-reliance and less susceptibility to changes in other income sources.

Employee Retention

The nonprofit sector often still struggles to adequately compensate its employees, which can lead to burnout in lower employees and vast salaries for top managers, and common sense would dictate fixing this problem. It is no secret that a not-for-profit employee is paid significantly less, and often works longer hours, than her counterpart in the for-profit sector. This is documented by Ann-Sophie Morrissette in the *Stanford Social Innovation Review*, where she lists improper compensation as one of the most common causes of burnout.[4]

Burnout causes employees to leave, which leaves holes in the organizations that need to be filled, which lead to costly searches for new employees, who then need to be trained. After all the time and resources spent finding and training a new employee, the person may also wind up leaving, due to the endemic problems that caused the previous employee's burnout. The not-for-profit sector needs to display more common sense by addressing the systematic problem of improper compensation for employees. When employees are properly valued (and so properly compensated), more money is saved in the long run for the good work of the nonprofit.

On the other hand, compensation of nonprofit CEOs and senior management needs to be kept in check lest it run rampant. While they typically do not make as much as their for-profit counterparts, these CEOs receive substantial compensation from their organizations. Although transparency is currently a large issue in the not-for-profit sector, the sector does not bear as much oversight from the IRS. Therefore it falls on the organizations to act prudently and to ensure that CEO compensation is regulated and checked in order to display good governance and accountability. According to the National Council of Nonprofits, the CEO's salary should be determined by an independent body, and a document should be compiled that details the process in full.[5]

Internal Policies and Transparency

Another practice that the not-for-profit sector needs to adopt to display common sense is to mandate internal controls, such as conflict-of-interest and whistleblower policies. Documents that feature this information should be easily accessible to the public. Nonprofits, by nature, are supported by the public's money, and their assets belong to the public, due to nondistribution constraints (which prevent an organization's net earnings or assets from being distributed to any individuals who oversee the organization). Governance and oversight on these organizations and their assets is handled by the IRS, but oversight can be minimal, and malpractices and improper management can fly under the radar. Therefore, the sector needs to drive its own efforts to expand transparency, accountability, and internal controls.

The tax-exemption form for many nonprofits has recently changed to include sections regarding governance, management, and transparency.[6] New questions address whether or not the organization has whistleblower policies to protect employees who expose illegal and unethical practices, if the organization has a written-document retention and destruction policy, and if a conflict-of-interest policy is in place. Although nonprofits are not legally bound by these "voluntary"[7] guidelines, the absence of any of these policies does raise concerns. Having these policies, and making such information readily available to the public, should become the standard for the not-for-profit sector.[8] Accountability is like sunlight, which can illuminate and disinfectant a potentially grimy situation—*before* it gets rancid.

At its core, the not-for-profit sector serves to address needs or gaps that people feel society is lacking. In turn, the public either supports them directly through donations or indirectly through grants and tax breaks. Without the for-profit motive, and entrusted with public money and assets, the not-for-profit sector needs to motivate *itself* to achieve prudent and ethical behavior. Again, common sense should be the guide, because common sense is good for *all* sectors of our economies. The changes proposed above, though certainly not the only available options, we think prescribe a series of achievable, reasonable actions. They would make a clear statement that the not-for-profit sector is cognizant of the value of the gifts it receives from the public and its generous donors and that it is up to the task of properly stewarding them for the common good.

NOTES

1. US Department of Commerce Bureau of Economic Analysis (BEA), "Table 1.3.5: Gross Value Added by Sector" (2016). Accessed November 30, 2016: www.bea.gov.
2. Brice McKeever, "The Nonprofit Sector in Brief 2015: Public Charities, Giving, and Volunteering," figure 2, *Urban Institute* (October 29, 2015). Accessed November 29, 2016: www.urban.org.
3. For an example, see "Blenheim Palace: Private Events, Conferences, and Meetings," Blenheim Palace Events Ebrochure. Accessed November 30, 2016: http://en.calameo.com.
4. See Ann-Sophie Morrissette, "Five Myths that Perpetuate Burnout across Nonprofits," *Stanford Social Innovation Review* (October 31, 2016). Accessed December 1, 2016: https://ssir.org.
5. See National Council of Nonprofits, "Executive Compensation: What Should a Nonprofit Pay Its Chief Executive?" Accessed December 2, 2016: www.councilofnonprofits.org.
6. See IRS, "Form 990: Return of Organization Exempt from Income Tax" (2016). Accessed December 2, 2016: www.irs.gov.

7. According to "Sarbanes-Oxley Act and Implications for Nonprofits," *Independent Sector*. Accessed November 29, 2016: www.independentsector.org.

8. For an example, see the website of the Oregon Shakespeare Festival: www. osfashland.org (we accessed December 1, 2016). Their "Financials & Bylaws" page demonstrates excellent transparency policies.

CHAPTER 14
LET MARKETS WORK

I t is common sense to follow the market. We live in a world that is built around markets, so it is sensible to give them the room and the support they need to work. In the process we all flourish.

Commodity markets are different than financial markets. Its beginnings trace to the north German town of Lübeck in the year 1159, and historians will recall the Hanseatic League, which dominated Baltic maritime trade from 1400 to 1750. The wonders of commodity markets are that when prices are high, markets attract capital and entrepreneurs to create surpluses and end the high prices. At the other end of the market, low prices tend to discourage capital and discourage innovation.

You read it every day, it seems. Here are just a few examples of the headlines and warnings you can find in the media decrying markets.

"World faces widespread food shortages."
"Crops to become scarce."
"Billions lack water."
"Natural resources in limited supply."
"Overconsumption strains resources."
"Overcoming energy crisis a must to ensure sustainable development."

These are actual news reports. None of this paints a very pretty picture of our world or our future, but it does not present a very accurate picture, either. If you look at the world around us, you see something very different—something that should make us much more optimistic about the world we live in and the world we are passing to future generations.

Commodity markets work better than any other approach we have encountered—better than the most well-intentioned efforts of government, or the most passionate efforts of even the most committed individuals and most energetic NGOs. Commodity markets are older than financial markets and much more efficient. They are based on a common-sense notion called "trading."

We continue to advance the use of markets for energy, water, and fuel. We must allow prices to be the allocator of resources, not the government. We also need to simplify the regulatory process for new plants and infrastructure; we must reduce the subsidies that distort markets. Believe it or not, in our lifetime we have actually never seen a completely free market.

An Abundance of Energy

Let's start by looking at the energy sector. Just how big is this so-called energy crisis we hear about?

The truth is the world is awash in energy.

In the United States, for example, our proven coal reserves dwarf our traditional annual consumption. We have an estimated 237 billion tons in the ground, but use one billion—or less—each year. The World Coal Association says we have proven global coal reserves sufficient to meet our demand for 110 years, at present consumption rates. They also point out that the technology exists to use coal for our utility and industrial needs and still meet highly ambitious targets in carbon-emission reduction.

If carbon-emission reduction is your big worry, then also remember that about one in five American households gets its power from nuclear plants. Today, 104 nuclear plants continue to operate and account for about 70 percent of America's emission-free power generation.

But we haven't built a nuclear plant in nearly fifty years. Most of us are old enough to remember Three Mile Island and Chernobyl and the Fukushima plant meltdown—and the chilling effects those events had on talk about the role of nuclear power in the energy mix.

But, when it comes to energy matters, we tend to think first about oil. Energy experts point to reserves of about 250 billion barrels of crude oil in both Russia and Saudi Arabia. Venezuela claims a top spot in the production tables, thanks to its considerable recent discoveries. A Norwegian energy consulting firm recently generated attention when it estimated US reserves at close to another quarter-trillion barrels—roughly half of it locked away in shale. Whatever source we choose to rely upon, the evidence is clear: We have extensive supplies of the various forms of petroleum we need—and will need.

In just three years, between June 2012 and June 2015, we saw US crude oil production rise by almost half, from about six million barrels per day to 9.6 million.

What drove such enormous growth? The market. Remember, much of the talk of the "energy crisis" can be traced back about fifteen years, when oil was trading as low as 20 dollars per barrel. When oil markets hit 100 dollars per barrel in October 2007 and then more than 140 dollars per barrel the next spring, investment in production began, and supplies started to take off. The market price for oil finally kicked in, as price exceeded subsidies and regulation costs.

In those intervening years, the US fracking industry came to life. We created more than 82,000 fracking wells in seventeen states, kick-starting a surge in supply.

Water, Water Everywhere

We see the same kind of picture in our focus on water. As many as 1.6 billion people live in areas that are "water scarce." Water-scarce areas promote illness, poverty, and ignorance.

How can such conditions exist, when our world is 87 percent water?

If we translate all that correctly, the important message involves water management far more than water shortage. Our focus should be on making sound decisions on water protection, use, and accessibility to those who need it for all their diverse needs. Once again, the market seems to me to be the logical vehicle for guiding that process.

Look at the work being done in places such as Singapore and Israel. Desalination projects there are helping create water surpluses where shortage and drought previously ruled. Israel's Sorek plant alone produces enough freshwater for one and a half million people. Other Israeli plants produce comparable amounts. Compare that aggressive approach of embracing science and technology to meet a pressing human need with the approach taken by some others.

Let's pick on California. There are serious water issues that face the Golden State—all man-made. See what has been done in Singapore and Israel with desalination, and you have to wonder how our California friends might benefit from a similar way of thinking.

Feeding a Growing World

The food sector may be more market-driven than many other parts of our economic system, But that's not to say market economics are allowed to flourish completely. The global food sector certainly has its share of market distortions. But market forces function sufficiently well to help build one of the most productive and extraordinary segments of our economy and our society.

We fail to appreciate what a remarkable food system we have. Today, we provide an abundant supply of food that is safer, more wholesome, more affordable, and more accessible than at any point in human history. We provide food for billions of people, including an estimated 75 million hungry new mouths every year. This system is capable not just of meeting our current enormous demand for food, but also of meeting substantial increases in food demand that lie ahead of us.

The world has enormous untapped potential for increases in productivity. Our future depends upon capitalizing on that potential. There aren't vast new areas of environmentally sustainable lands to be brought into production.

The initial resistance to GMOs is giving way to a more reasoned way of thinking. The truth is, we need to apply those innovations in science to advance a second generation of green revolution. We need to unlock the power of genetics, to create the productivity increases needed. The new frontiers of genetics will be crucial to boosting our global productive capacity, and to protecting the natural resource base on which the future depends.

We have to move beyond a romanticized notion of a farm life based on 40 acres and a mule. For instance, milk cow productivity. If milk cow productivity in the rest of the world would reach US equivalents, we would be awash in milk. The same holds true for corn, soybeans, and wheat. There are many instances where the use of current technology can help increase food surpluses.

We could talk about the importance of trade in making markets work. We could talk about the emerging information age, and the way the digital world is changing the agricultural world. We could talk about changing dietary patterns, or the debate over climate change. But the biggest threat to our ability to meet rising demand for basic necessities like energy, water and food is *ourselves*.

Witness the enormous creativity and productive capacity of human beings around the world. There is no end to what we can accomplish when allowed to use our intellect and experience. It is all about the right incentives. The power of the market, when allowed to work, is compelling.

It is also clear what happens when we distort and restrict the incentives created by a functioning market: we stifle our capacity to create and to produce.

Most often, we distort markets with the best of intentions. We want to protect a given interest, or to advance some policy goal. But along the way, the imperfect judgments of politicians, bureaucrats, regulators, and other well-intentioned people have detrimental effects on our real best interests.

For a truly frightening example of what can happen from market distortion, simply look to Venezuela right now. Its attempts to manage the market have produced dramatic food shortages. People line up for hours, hoping that something—anything—will be available. Fighting and food riots have become regular worries. It may be an extreme example of what can happen when we stray too far from market realities, but it is worth noting.

Let's hope such a situation never materializes anywhere else, for that matter. Our simple, common-sense advice on how to avoid such a calamity is much like the ancient demand made by Moses to pharaoh in arguing for a better future for the Israelites: "Let my people go."

To build a secure future for humankind, our plea is this: "let markets work." That is common-sense business.

CHAPTER 15

THE FUTURE OF COMMON-SENSE BUSINESS

That's the way things come clear. All of a sudden. And then you realize how obvious they've been all along.
—Madeleine L'Engle

"Green shoots" usually refer to plant growth, but in recent years, the term has come to have a second meaning in economic life. Everyone from the minister of trade and industry in the UK to the chair of the US Federal Reserve Bank seems to be using the term to suggest that the economy is improving. This new meaning—signs of economic recovery based on real and positive data in a downturn—is a cause for hope and an expectation for a better future on the immediate horizon.

We want to steal the phrase and apply it to common-sense business that is prudent, sustainable, and oriented to stewardship, as we have been unwinding the storyline in the chapters of this book. Could it be that in this arena, we are seeing evidence of springtime? Do you hear Aaron Copland's *Appalachian Spring* starting up?

Thomas Blackburn's famous poem, "An Easter Hymn," sums it up best:

Awake, thou wintry earth—
Fling off thy sadness!
Fair vernal flowers, laugh forth,
Your ancient gladness.

Could it be that we are turning the corner, that some companies—increasingly more companies, and across many distant lands—have learned the painful lessons of casting off common sense and are again (just) starting to practice the virtues we have been here extolling? Are there also new companies, startups, and social ventures that give rise to the very same theme? If so, we should be rejoicing and applaud their efforts while insisting that still more forces join their ranks. We are not home yet.

There is a group in Toronto with the curious name "Corporate Knights" that defines this trend and studies it every year. They define what we call common-sense business in their own way: "recognition that long-term interests are intellectually and financially consistent with resource efficiency, proactive health and safety, and responsible leadership." To put it in simple terms even a fifth grader can understand, these kinds of companies create more wealth than they destroy.

This group recently announced the *Global 100 Most Sustainable Companies*. Their methodology is sound, based on empirically respectable and objective data samples, and they appear to have done their homework. Here's their top ten:

- **Umicore**, a Belgian materials-technology company, has developed "The Umicore Way" around vision, values, and organizational principles on sustainable development.
- **Natura Cosmetics** is the first company from Brazil to join the Business Transparency Program.
- **Statoil**, a Norwegian oil and gas firm, has witnessed outstanding achievements by its employees and contractors in health, safety, and environmental management.
- **Neste Oil**, from Finland, offers cleaner traffic fuel solutions.
- **Novo Nordisk**, the Danish pharmaceutical company, has adopted triple bottom line (TBL) and ties its long-term business success to a healthy economy and environment.

- **Storebrand**, a financial services company from Norway, has made great strides in green life insurance and pensions.
- **Philips Electronics** from the Netherlands helps its suppliers achieve better sustainability in the health care, consumer lifestyle, and lighting segments where it operates.
- **Biogen Idec**, the oldest biotech company in the United States, focuses on its corporate citizenship—improving lives, rethinking resources, and creating value.
- **Dassault Systems**, from France, in aviation, was recognized for its 3-D imaging of sustainable innovations.
- **Westpac Bank**, an Australian banking giant, was listed for its sustainable strategy, which entails principles for doing business in governance and ethics, customer and employee practices for conservation and the environment, and consumer involvement and supply-chain management.

If you scan the longer list, you find lots of big, well-known companies who have fashioned sustainable businesses, or models, or units in divisions and are making real headway. Some of those names include: Intel, BMW, Adidas, Cisco, Daiwa, Alcatel, Siemens, BASF, Clorox, Daimler, Vale, GE, Henkel, SAP, NEC, and Campbell's.

Is prudent business, oriented in common sense, experiencing a renaissance? The trend seems to be growing daily. Perhaps we are seeing more than a blip on the radar. Actual good habits may be forming around the values and ideas we have been advocating in this book. Common sense may be taking hold.

There is no reason for irrational exuberance or misplaced confidence, but there is now considerable optimism about changed companies that set the pace for still other companies and even entire industries.

Recall that at the turn of the last century, everyone was gaga about what was called e-business. The bricks and mortar would fall away, and only digital enterprises would survive, we were told. Everything had to relate to the Internet or it was instantly considered dead in the water. Well, what happened in a few short years? E-business itself became part and parcel of *every* business. E-business doesn't even really exist any longer as a stand-alone phenomenon. All business has evolved to incorporate the new digital models and technologies. Perhaps the same thing is happening with common sense, sustainable business?

The Guardian newspaper in the UK believes so, as they have started an ongoing series on sustainable case studies, which we can all learn from. They break sustainable practices into clear categories: Net Positive, Natural Capital, Biodiversity, Built Environment, Carbon, Collaboration, Communicating, Consulting, Energy and Carbon Management, Engaging Employees, Social Impact, Supply Chain, Waste, Water, and Work. This is a fairly comprehensive pulse of things that are happening and "snowballing," to use another fashionable term, as the idea and practice of sustainable business takes hold and spreads. From where we sit in the academy, in think tanks, doing policy research and advising companies of every size from around the world, we observe the following three trends, or macro-drivers, which give us real cause for hope.

First, sustainable goods and services are growing exponentially. Best estimates suggest that by next year (2017), that part of the global economy will be $10 trillion. Put bluntly, the C-suite has started to embrace this reality. Second, sustainability supports lower prices and drives down business costs. Even Wal-Mart is doing it! By reducing waste and making companies more efficient in product design, we all benefit. Think of Starbucks switching to recyclable cups; it certainly didn't keep us out of Starbucks. But it kept more Starbucks out of the landfill.

And last, and perhaps most powerfully, consumers themselves want real and lasting change. Seventy-four percent of Americans now believe that climate change is harmful, and the number is higher in Europe. As a result, more and more consumers around the globe are demanding that companies take steps to embrace conservation and install more prudent measures.

Green shoots are appearing everywhere, and over time they will blossom into full-grown plants and trees, then into thick forests, altering our existence for the better. Common sense may slowly be rising back up from the ashes.

EPILOGUE

As we have established, common sense is for business, and business excels when common-sense actions are accepted practice. Simply put, people flourish, companies grow, economies thrive, and nations improve, because business and society are intertwined. Hopefully, you have come to a similar conclusion and now seek to bring common sense to your job, to your workplace, and to our broader economy.

But common sense isn't only for business.

As a kind of practical wisdom, grounded in the virtue of prudence, common sense is for all of life—everywhere and at all times. We live in a turbulent and uncertain age of constant betterment brought about by specialization, collaboration, and a sustained upsurge in the discovery of new and useful knowledge and technologies. Yet even before Adam Smith penned *The Wealth of Nations* in 1776, he wrote a much more important book, *The Theory of Moral Sentiments*, wherein he argued for such common sense. The notions of benevolence and sympathy were rooted in a moral philosophy where economic activity combined the best head with the best heart. Mind and soul were not separated but united. Reason and faith were two sides of the same coin.

The operative tide in the picture painted by Smith was a "commercial republic"—a society of liberty fashioned through trade and commerce to advance individual well-being materially, intellectually, aesthetically, and morally. Commerce and governance were the twin pillars of the common good. While commercial activity was paramount, the common-sense mentality held implications for all the mediating institutions of civil society—wherever life was experienced together—families, churches, voluntary associations, schools, and universities. The dominant cultural values of this commercial republic include enterprise, self-governance, collaboration, subsidiarity, and patriotism. Such a collaborative and democratic state witnesses liberty for all; freedom in speech, thought, and religion; and property protected by the rule of law—all informed by the common-sense, learn-by-doing virtues of self-governed persons.

* * *

As we have proposed, the overwhelming processes of modernization, globalization, and digitization are putting to the test our experiment in self-governance. The affiliated organizations so critical to its success have too frequently been abandoned or ignored. Business, however, remains the first among equals in our materialistic and acquisitive societies. It is necessary therefore to bring common sense back *especially* in the realm of business so that it can be rekindled as well in every corner of society and for the common good. (Common sense and the common good are, in fact, joined together. You can't have one without the other. You can't sustain one without the other.)

As for our home nation of the United States, the notion that business practitioners should play a significant role in the development of the country can be attributed to the common sense and fortitude of the many businessmen and women in the nation's very founding—notably Benjamin Franklin, George Mason, Samuel Adams, John Hancock, Betsy Ross, Robert Morris, and George Washington himself. These revolutionaries understood full well the necessary sequence of business success and the spirit needed to achieve national well-being. Their practical insights and wisdom, combined with the scholarship of their more youthful collaborators such as Thomas Jefferson and John Jay, led to a national celebration of individual autonomy, inclusion, and free markets. Such collaborative endeavors positioned business and its practitioners as valued actors in the process of building a nation and forging a just society. Businesspersons went beyond wealth creation, and even invention, to engage in all industries and in every part of the nation. Their accomplishments in national governance and in philanthropy have arguably been exceptional in all of recorded history. We would go so far as to say that the growth, wealth, and prosperity of America came about in large part because of common-sense business.

It continues to this day, but it is under threat.

As Thomas Paine advised in his original and timely tract, with which we began this book, we need American independence and the health of a society founded in the business of common sense. We cannot let our forms and organs of governance drift toward an administrative or authoritarian state. This departure from the nation's traditional scheme of governance as a collaborative democratic republic would spell our demise, if not our doom.

So with Paine we are proud to end in restatement: "Society is produced by our wants, and government by wickedness; the former promotes our happiness positively by uniting our affections, the latter negatively by restraining our vices. The one encourages intercourse, the other creates distinctions. The first is a patron, the last a punisher."

Tradition tells of a chime that changed the entire world when it rang on July 8, 1776. It was the sound from the tower of Independence Hall summoning the citizens of Philadelphia to hear the first public reading of the Declaration of Independence by Colonel John Nixon. The Pennsylvania Assembly had ordered the Bell in 1751 to commemorate the fiftieth anniversary of William Penn's 1701 Charter of Privileges, Pennsylvania's original constitution. It spoke of the rights and freedoms valued by people the world over. Particularly insightful were Penn's ideas on religious freedom, his stance on American rights, and his inclusion of citizens in enacting laws. The Liberty Bell gained iconic importance when abolitionists, in their efforts to put an end to slavery throughout America, adopted it as a symbol. As the Bell was created to commemorate the golden anniversary of Penn's Charter, the inscription of "Proclaim Liberty throughout all the land unto all the inhabitants thereof," taken from Leviticus 25:10, seemed particularly apt.

We believe we need to ring that same bell again, to defend and rearticulate our call to common sense.

Toward this end, we have taken you on a tour of common-sense thinking—both ancient, modern, and up-and-coming. We've demonstrated both what common sense has to offer to business and how in modern-day economics, common-sense thinking as a virtue has declined. We've looked at how we can restore prudent, sensible reasoning to our prevailing economic theories and our ideas about corporate agency, governance, and responsibility. We've challenged you to turn the idea of the modern corporation on its head, calling firms to contribute to, not suck the life out of, the benefits and beauty among us.

We've shared a number of truly fascinating cases from Canada, Germany, Japan, Great Britain, India, China, and the United States and across various industries, from energy to agriculture to tech to retail. We've offered you some very useable tools—tools we ourselves use—a matrix of virtuous actions, a protocol on enterprise-wide risk management, and three audits that (if you take the time and study the gaps in your company's performance) will make your company better and more prudent. We've even given you an insider's peek into Whitney's company and the common-sense values that make it strong. It would be commonsensical to make good use of it all, like the new "green shoots" we highlighted, which suggest there is indeed a way back to prudence and that ever more companies are already traveling down the ecologically and economically more sustainable path.

Without the four Ps of common-sense business—prudence, patience, principles, and practicality—capitalism will falter and decay. It needs a moral framework and wise institutions to sustain it. Will you, can you, ought you make the changes that are necessary? Will you keep doing what you are doing, or will you reorient to a more sustainable business future? What difference could your firm make for the common good of your community, your nation, even your planet? We started this book with an obituary for common sense. Now we're challenging you to breathe life back into this virtue again—through the best chance we have: business.

Index